A Collection of Writings by

Ray Alton

TO LIVE IS

Christ

*To Encourage Total Dependence on Christ
in the Moment By Moment Journey of Life*

Cover design by Bill Weaver
Editing by Diane Mattingly
Printed by Instantpublisher.com

TO LIVE IS CHRIST
A COLLECTION OF WRITINGS BY RAY ALTON
Copyright © 2004 by Linda Alton
Published by Higher Image Ministries, Inc.
Flowery Branch, GA 30542

ISBN 0-9753749-0-7

Printed in the United States of America.

*Dedicated to and
in memory of Ray,*

*my gift from God
and love of my heart,
whose authentic life was an
inspiration and encouragement
to me and so many others
to be who God created us to be.*

ACKNOWLEDGMENTS

I could not complete this book and leave out this page. My appreciation and thanks must be expressed to all the people who have been such an encouragement while working on this project. To my family: you are a part of what is written on these pages because you walked the journey with us while we were learning the truths shared here. Your love and support along the way is worth more than gold. To my friends: you have cried with me, laughed with me, given me hugs, time, and a listening ear. Putting this book together has been a new adventure and you have cheered me on when I was unsure of my next move. Thank you for being there. To Bill and Dee Dee: you did an awesome job. Thank you for helping make this book a reality. To Carolyn and Willette: Thank you for doing the proofreading and catching my mistakes. You helped put on the finishing touches. To my Abba Father: you are my joy, my peace, my comfort, my life. You gave me the vision for this book and have used it in my healing process, taking me deeper in my dependence on You. I will forever love You and give You praise.

From a heart full of love,
Linda

CONTENTS

FOREWARD

Throughout a person's lifetime, we all meet a lot of people. Of that group, some become our friends. Out of that smaller number, we will meet a very few number of people who impact our lives in transformational ways. Ray Alton was a man like that.

I first met Ray in 1990, shortly after I had come to understand my identity in Christ. I was immediately captivated by him. Ray Alton was the personification of the phrase "wit and wisdom." His sense of humor and his insight into the depths of our life in Christ were combined in a way that made him a magnetic person. People were always attracted to Ray.

As a grace neophyte, I found myself irresistibly drawn to him. I bought many a lunch for Ray just so I could spend one on one time with him, picking his brain, asking him how to apply grace to my life and ministry which had run on a legalistic track for a lifetime. His answers were always on the mark. He helped shape my thinking in those early days of my grace walk.

Ray impacted untold numbers of people through his teaching and discipleship. I am thrilled to see his ministry continued through this book. I believe the Holy Spirit had Ray write these things because He knew that after he went home, this would be a way for him to continue to impact lives.

As you read this book, you'll recognize Ray's voice. These pages have the same wit and wisdom that supernaturally poured from him during his lifetime. I won't promise that the book won't make you miss Ray. But I will promise you that reading it will make you love Jesus more. That was Ray's gift in this world and that gift now goes on working through the pages that follow.

Read *To Live Is Christ* and walk with Jesus. You can expect to find a smile coming to your face some times, a tear coming to your eyes at others, and a sense of the Holy Spirit speaking to you on every page.

Dr. Steve McVey
President, Grace Walk Ministries
Internationally known author and speaker

INTRODUCTION

This book is the fulfillment of a dream. My husband Ray loved writing and had dreamed of writing a book for many years. He was encouraged for a long time by many people, especially me, to give it a go and had finally decided if he was ever going to do it, now was the time. But before this dream became a reality he finished his race here on earth. As it says in 2 Timothy 4, he fought the good fight, finished the course, kept the faith, and was awarded the crown of righteousness by his Lord. He is now part of the "great cloud of witnesses" spoken of in Hebrews 12:1, cheering us on to run our race with endurance.

The day after Ray went to Heaven I found a personal journal entry he had written on his computer three months earlier. He was writing about a conversation we had earlier that evening. You see, Ray was a veteran teacher and speaker and I had just begun to step into that arena. We were leaving Virginia in a couple of days moving back to Georgia, following God's leading to launch a new ministry – Higher Image Ministries. I expected as we got started that Ray's schedule would immediately fill up with invitations. Instead he got sick soon after we moved and didn't speak or teach publicly again. Though he had no idea what was ahead of us when he wrote these words, God knew and realized what I would need to hear the morning I read the following:

"Our newsletter went out last week. As a result,

Linda was asked to speak at a women's retreat of 28 women. She was so excited and a bit chagrined. She was not expecting to be asked to do ministry before me, but she was. In fact, she was enthusiastically asked!

"Why should I be the first one asked to speak?"
"Why not?" I asked.

WE are beginning a new ministry together. So, why not? I'm certainly not jealous. I'm excited for her and for us. I've always known she has a ministry that is hers between her and our Father. She need never ride on my coattails to do ministry.

Because of what is in her heart, I expect her to be quite busy."

This was the first thing Father used to reveal His direction for what would come next in my life. I knew beyond any doubt that I was to go forward with Higher Image Ministries. It had been a vision given by Father to both Ray and me. I still had the same ministry and now had Ray's story to tell as well. Many other things followed to confirm this direction for me, even to this day.

A couple of days after finding Ray's journal entry Father added something new to my ministry vision. Having files and notebooks full of various things Ray had written over the years that were filled with insight, encouragement, and challenge, the book that he dreamed of writing was already in my possession. I was given the vision to compile some of his writings into what you now hold in your hands. I knew that doing this would help me heal from my loss as I read through his material, make it possible for his teaching to continue to minister to people for years to come, and make Ray's dream come true.

So as you read this selection of writings I pray that the words that Ray wrote during his spiritual journey will encourage you in your own.

Gracefully yours,

Linda Alton

1

MAN'S PURPOSE

Even though I have logged quite a few miles in my Christian journey and have learned much of God's truth, I still have uncomfortable moments when I ask, "Now what's this all about? Why are we doing this?" I think everyone needs a reality check now and then to keep them on track. What does "on track" mean and better yet, what track are you on? Do you have purpose to your life? What is your purpose? Why are you here? If you know what it is, are you going about it deliberately? If you don't know what it is, do you even want to know? Have you ever given it much thought?

Even if you want to start thinking about your purpose do you know where to begin looking for the answers? Are you stuck aimlessly following the rut you've been walking in for a while, pounding out the humdrum of a survival mentality never looking to the left or right because adding thoughts beyond the rut would be too painful or too overwhelming?

Do you ever ask yourself, "What is this all about anyway and what is my part in it?" How important is it that we just work, buy houses, make payments on cars, make more babies, try to maintain families and maybe have trusted Christ as our Savior? And if we have trusted Christ, why would we not all quit our jobs and run without restraint up to every person we can find and warn them of sin and hell and then tell them of the glory of salvation?

Why would God not want us to abandon everything and just tell folks about Jesus? What's up with farms, jobs, houses, cars, stores, roads, sports, vacations, spouses, children, and all the other things about which we make life? Why are most of our waking hours spent on making money and buying things all the while putting more and more time, energy, and money into maintaining our possessions? Why do we even concern ourselves with owning anything, protecting anything or improving anything when they will not endure the fire anyway?

We get heaven when we die, right? We'll have all we need there, right? Then why is all the mental, emotional and physical energy of our lives spent on the temporal? Well, from our perspective, discomfort is to be avoided and comfort is coveted. It feels good to have, protect and improve our existence on planet earth. We feel pain and pressure in the here and now so we want those things to go away, now. We want to be cool when we're hot, warm when we're cold, happy when we're sad, well when we're sick, and secure when we're fearful.

The temporal things in our lives command our time, energy and money because we desire comfort. But if this world were made totally comfortable, we wouldn't need God, would we? God didn't make earth to replace Himself. Nothing in creation was intended to completely satisfy us. Look at us. We're off exploring the vastness of the universe and I guarantee you that if someone finds the edge of the universe, someone else will be right behind trying to figure out some way to discover what lies beyond.

Man was created to realize and experience God. Man was created in such a way that nothing outside of God, nothing above, on or within the earth was designed to fully satisfy man. There are consistent obstacles to every pursuit that leads man away from God. God made us and put us on His earth in His universe. He has all the answers. I do not, nor have I heard any theologian or scholar give answers that satisfied me completely.

If neither this earth nor our universe was created to meet all our wants and needs, then does it make sense that God intends for us to be satisfied with Himself? It appears that He will first let us either reach a place of discomfort and cry out for the lack of temporal means or discover the emptiness within the glut of acquired temporal means in order to discover that we were made to need Him and Him alone. God created a longing inside each of us and a need inside each of us for more than we can see, touch, taste, smell, or hear.

What is our purpose? It is to discover and embrace God through His Son, Jesus Christ, and yield to Him in order for His life to be expressed through us. It makes no difference where we are on this earth or what we are doing. Our purpose remains the same. Have you met Him?

2

HAVE YOU SEEN HIS GRACE?

My wife, Linda, and I used to own a house on a wooded lot in Marietta, Georgia. One year a blue jay decided to build her nest in the angle of the downspout next to our driveway. She determined that where the gutter touched the brick was a perfect place to build a nest.

I could have torn the nest down at any time but I didn't. The bird probably thought it was her ability to protect the nest that prevented me from removing it. The truth is that it was my grace toward her and her family that kept me from destroying the fragile nest, not her ability to protect it.

The bird, possibly prideful in the performance of its duty to protect, will never know of my grace but she still experienced it. She didn't have to understand my grace or even ask for it in order to benefit from it. It was my choice to extend it to her.

How many times has God allowed you to think that you controlled a situation or a person or even yourself and you came away thinking you could protect, provide or escape very well in your own strength? During those times you may never have realized His grace towards you. Will you now become aware of God's deep love and grace? Can you now look back and see the hand of God on a past situation or relationship?

Who is better able to protect you and those you love? Who is better able to overthrow your enemies? Who is more able to meet all of your needs? Is it you or is it the God of all grace?

And after you have suffered a little while,
the God of all grace, who called you to His
eternal glory in Christ, will Himself perfect,
confirm, strengthen and establish you.
I Peter 5:10

Unless the Lord builds the house, they
labor in vain who build it; unless the
Lord guards the city, the watchman
keepsawake in vain. It is vain for you to
rise up early, to retire late, to eat the bread
of painful labors: For He gives to His
beloved even in his sleep.
Psalms 127:1, 2

3

TEMPTATION VERSUS VICTORY

How would you define temptation and victory? Read the following statements and answer *true* or *false*:

- You can be a mature believer and yet continue to be tempted in the areas in which you've always been tempted.
- A mature believer is one who is consistently free from temptation.
- Temptations originate from your own thoughts.
- It is normal for believers to be tempted.
- Temptation in my thoughts is sin.
- You can't have true victory over temptation in this life.
- Victory means that I'm no longer tempted.
- Victory is the result of success over each test, temptation, or trial.
- Victory is living rightly each moment of every day.
- God never leads anyone into temptation.

Are your definitions the same or are they different? Let's look at some scripture and see if we can get a clearer picture of temptation and victory. One of the best places to begin is with the temptations Christ Himself endured. Satan was given permission to fire the first shots between himself and Jesus. Watch how he couches his temptation.

Luke 4:1-3 *Jesus, full of the Holy Spirit, returned from the Jordan and was led about by the Spirit in the wilderness for forty days, being tempted by the devil. And He ate nothing during those days, and when they had ended, He became hungry. And the devil said to Him, "If You are the Son of God, tell this stone to become bread."*

He didn't say, "If you are hungry, turn the stone into bread." This phrasing would have been aimed only at meeting Jesus' immediate need to ease His hunger. Instead, he said, "If You are the Son of God." What is really being attacked in this temptation? Satan is trying to get Jesus to doubt His identity. "If you are who you say you are, then, meet your need." This was a temptation to use who He was to meet a genuine need, but independent of God. Have you ever been there? Have you ever experienced a need but were actually challenged on your worth, security, or competency to meet that need?

Luke 4:4-7 *And Jesus answered him, "It is written, 'man shall not live on bread alone.' And he led Him up and showed Him all the kingdoms of the world in a moment of time. And the devil said to Him, 'I will give You all this domain and its glory; for it has been handed over to me, and I give it to whomever I wish. Therefore if You worship before me, it shall all be Yours.'"*

In this instance, Satan is challenging Jesus with a temptation concerning what He has because of who He is. Knowing who He was and knowing that God would accomplish what He sent Him to do, Jesus answered, *"You shall worship the Lord your God and serve Him only."*

Luke 4:8. Jesus valued serving God God's way above all offers of short cuts or exchanges. Jesus was intent on doing only what His Father said. He was predetermined in His answer. Do you have a ready answer for temptation?

Then Satan tempted Jesus one more time concerning His identity. Luke 4:9-12 says, *And he led Him to Jerusalem and had Him stand on the pinnacle of the temple, and said to Him, "If You are the Son of God, throw Yourself down from here; for it is written, 'He will command His angels concerning you to guard you,' and, 'on their hands they will bear you up, so that you will not strike your foot against a stone.'" Jesus answered, "It is said, 'you shall not put the Lord your God to the test.'"* Jesus didn't have to prove to Satan or anyone who He was. Neither Satan nor us can force God into a test or temptation to prove Himself to gain our acceptance of Him in order for Him to be okay. Never has, never will. Satan wants you to fall for the same ploy, to prove you are who you say you are.

Luke 4:13 *When the devil had finished every temptation, he left Him until an opportune time.* What a statement to take home with you! When is it most opportune to hit you with a temptation to trust yourself, to act independent, and to sin? When you are already down. So, when do you see Christ down? On the cross. Let's go there now.

Luke 23:35 *And the people stood by, looking on. And even the rulers were sneering at Him, saying, "He saved others; let Him save Himself if this is the Christ of God, His Chosen One."* "IF" this is the Christ of God. Here again Jesus was tempted to prove who He is and to act independently of God. This time, instead of being blatantly visible, Satan is working through people over whom Jesus wept as He looked out over Jerusalem, people whom He loved.

Luke 23:36-37 *The soldiers also mocked Him, coming up to Him, offering Him sour wine, and saying, "If You are the King of the Jews, save Yourself!"* Here we move down one rung on the social ladder to the soldiers who enforced Roman rule over the Jews. Even they taunted Jesus, tempting Him to prove who He was.

What comes next in this test would cut to the heart of any leader, any Christian worker or anyone who wants to serve God. Luke 23:38-39 *Now there was also an inscription above Him, "THIS IS THE KING OF THE JEWS." One of the criminals who were hanged there was hurling abuse at Him, saying, "Are You not the Christ? Save Yourself and us!"* This time Jesus is challenged to prove who He is by saving Himself and further challenged to fulfill His mission to man by operating outside of God's method and timing. "Aren't You really who You say You are? Aren't You here to save us? Then do something about it! Prove it to us!"

Jesus either addressed the temptation with truth from scripture or merely rejected the temptation as a lie. Either way sets a good example to follow. Take the thought captive. Ask yourself, "What need would entertaining that temptation meet for me?" Just as Christ was attacked at the need of hunger, what need was the basis of sin's temptation to me? What area of my identity was attacked? Was it my worth? My security? My competency? Stand and rest on the truth. Tell yourself the truth of where these identity issues have already been met. Do I have to be "in Christ" and have what the temptation offered me to stop the fear, hurt or pressure in order for me to be okay? The answer quite simply is NO. Christ is my life and Christ alone is what or Who makes me okay.

I am free in Him. Galatians 5:1 *It was for freedom that Christ set us free; therefore keep standing firm and do not be subject again to a yoke of slavery.*

I am made perfect in Him. Ephesians 4:23-24 *And that you be renewed in the spirit of your mind and put on the new self, which in the likeness of God has been created in Holiness and righteousness of the truth.*

I am complete in Him. Colossians 2:9-10 *For in Him all the fullness of Deity dwells in bodily form, and in Him you have been made complete.*

In Him I am equipped and ready to face whatever comes at me in this life. 2 Peter 1: 3 *...seeing that His divine power has granted to us everything pertaining to life and godliness, through the true knowledge of Him who called us by His own glory and excellence.*

So, what is victory? Can I really have victory over those things that tempt me? Is true victory an event or could it be that true victory is a Person? Do you want to experience a few more events of victory than events of defeat or do you want to know you have Victory because Christ is your Victory now and forever?

Victory is a person, not an event. Victory is resting in who you are in Him no matter what sin, Satan and the world's value system tries to sell you to meet your needs. Victory is Christ! And if you are in Him, victory is yours!

For the law of the Spirit of life in Christ Jesus has set you free from the law of sin and of death.
Romans 8:2

4

THE UNRELENTING PULL OF SIN

I used to believe, and sometimes even taught, that the more that you rest in Christ, the less intense is the temptation of sin. Temptation has a magnetic draw that confines you under its power when you get too close. Consider the alcoholic who drives around the liquor store seven or eight times claiming 1 Corinthians 10:13. He plays near its lure to the point that he succumbs to the urge to stop, get out of his car, get money out of the automatic teller machine, go back to the liquor store, get out of his car, go in, choose his poison, pay for it, leave, go somewhere behind a closed door, open the bottle, open his mouth, raise his hand and then claim Scripture? Not!

There is a point where you claim truth and stand on the side of freedom. There is also a point where you are so convinced that the sin will meet your immediate need that God will let you experience the full consequences of your getting too close to sin's gravity. If you are determined to meet your needs through sin, I believe He will let you go and even release you from the pain of fighting your own conscience.

This raises an interesting question. I see some people who DO NOT *condemn themselves in that which they allow* as stated in Romans 14. They assume that because their conscience has cleared, that it must now be "okay." In reality, it still isn't okay. It will never be okay. What the person is experiencing is the release from the pull of the Holy Spirit. If you've just got to have "this thing," God will let you experience the whole deal, death and all.

This raises another question. Did God say it was okay? Is God sanctioning what you've chosen to use to meet your need? No. What God is doing is "letting you hit the wall," however long it takes. This is not where you want to be. It isn't even close. At the point of this depth of deception, it will take a major blow to come back into reality. This point of deception can go as far as to say that not only has God sanctioned it, but also that He is responsible for providing it; that it's a gift. I don't think so!

Do I believe that the intensity of the temptation to sin grows weaker the more I rest in Christ as my sufficiency in having met all of my needs? I don't anymore. At one time, this would be how I had explained it to myself, but this is a lie. Sin and its temptation do not grow weaker in intensity. Just like gravity, sin's temptation is just as intense now as it was before I knew truth.

The gravitational pull of the earth doesn't change. The pull at sea level is always the same. The pull at ten miles high is always the same and the pull from one hundred thousand miles out is and will remain the same.

But the pull at zero FEELS different than the pull at one hundred thousand miles. This feeling is why I assumed that it was a weakening of the temptation itself but the different intensities at the different levels always remains the same. So what is the application here?

What I discovered is that resting in the law of the Spirit of life in Christ moves me "out" as I trust moment by moment in its truth. When my eyes are on me, I come dangerously close to crashing into temptation or actually do. When my eyes have abandoned all else but Him, I soar effortlessly through the universe. The whole point of this article is to warn you not to ever think that sin, or its power to tempt, is weakened by the sight of your faith in Christ. Remember what God told Cain in Genesis 4, *...sin is crouching at the door and its desire is for you.* Sin is at full power ready to push open any door not secured by resting, believing and acting on God's truth.

So, don't get cocky about the victories you've experienced over sinful habits, thoughts or behaviors. Landing on purpose or crashing doesn't take very long but the effects or consequences could last a lifetime. Don't be lulled into a false sense of security thinking that you are winning over sin and that sin has weakened in your experience. Rest, believe and act on God's truth knowing that your victory and security is found in Christ alone.

*"Father, I desire that they also, whom
Thou hast given Me, be with Me where I am."*
John 17:24a

5

DESIRED
BY CHRIST

I've known for many years that I was a "whosoever" (John 3:16) because one day I prayed and received Christ as my Savior. Years later I learned that God had also made me righteous, that I am totally acceptable and lovable to Him, and that I am completely forgiven. These realizations were life changing.

Learning to accept my acceptance and learning that there wasn't anything I could do to make myself more righteous or more acceptable to God led to my realization that the finished work of Christ is also the basis upon which I could accept myself. This brought peace, trust, and a willingness to risk obeying God along with freedom from the bondage of a chronic, sinful, and guilt-ridden life. Wow! But wait, there's more!

A sermon I once gave ended with an examination of the prayer of Christ in John 17. I haven't been the same since! How many times have I read this passage? But this time Christ's own words jumped off the page at me like never before!

In verse 24 Jesus tells God that He desires us to be with Him in His restored glory. We are not just "whosoevers" to be checked off Jesus' to-do list. We are desired, wanted, valued, and friends in our Savior's eyes and heart. As Sally Field said when she won her Oscar, "You like me! You really like me!"

In His own words He likes and loves us much more than we can imagine or think! He knew all the stupid stuff we would do even after the point of our salvation. Even knowing that we would fall, He still died over 2,000 years ago to pay for it all and He still desires us to be with Him in glory! Where can man go to get another deal like that? Nowhere!

6

FREEDOM

Freedom is a word that is on many people's lips. For those who have been in bondage, the birth of freedom is a time of joy and a time to celebrate. But for many, when the celebration is winding down, the question comes, "Now what?"

Christians who taste freedom from legalism and freedom from sin for the first time can become anxious over what to "do now." Since they have never experienced this freedom before, being led only by the Holy Spirit and trusting His guidance alone is something new. The only thing they've known is bondage to rules, traditions, standards, and expectations placed on them by others as well as themselves.

It only makes sense. When you don't know who you are you will have no clue as to how to act. If God has brought you to an understanding of freedom in Christ and you are not sure where to go from there, take heart. He is not expecting you to know. That's why the Spirit of the Living God is in you - to show you who He is, who you are, to share a relationship with you, and to guide you in your walk.

Don't set your eyes on the world trying to figure out how you are now supposed to relate to it. Turn and face Him alone. Let Him draw you into deeper intimacy with Him. The noise in your head and heart will begin to subside and you will hear His Spirit speaking to you, guiding you through the circumstances of life.

I am the good shepherd; and I know My own,
and My own know Me,
John 10:14

My sheep hear my voice, and I know them
and they follow Me;
John 10:27

7

PROBLEMS

I wonder how much television has shaped how we think about resolving problems. Think about it. In the first five minutes of a typical TV show you are presented with an insurmountable challenge or catastrophe. Even considering the time it takes to run the commercials, all of the problems are resolved within thirty minutes or an hour.

I suspect that most of us have had God under our own law that requires Him to resolve our problems in the same way. Am I right? As soon as pain or suffering hits, we immediately call on God to relieve whatever it is that is causing our discomfort so that we can re-enter our comfort zone. We have mistakenly thought that this relief spelled victory and proved God's love for us.

I propose that rather than immediately praying for relief that we first thank God for the problem. You heard me correctly. Thank God for the problem. Ephesians 5:20 says, "...*giving thanks for all things in the name of our Lord Jesus Christ to God, even the Father*". Then let us thank Him for being in it with us. Psalms 46:1 says, "*God is our refuge and strength, a very present help in trouble.*"

Next, thank Him for the growth that will come

from being willing to not be in control and to let Christ live His life in and through you in the midst of your pain. Romans 8:20 - 21 says, *"For the creation was subjected to futility, not of its own will, but because of Him who subjected it, in hope that the creation itself also will be set free from its slavery to corruption into the freedom of the glory of the children of God."*

I have seen in my own life and in the lives of others that God is more interested in whose life is being expressed during a problem than in just relieving or resolving the problem itself. Many times God wants us to discover His love and victory within the situation, not apart from it. This realization has helped me to face life's issues confident in God's love and sovereignty rather than by using my own strength to defend against them.

8

WAXING
THE DEAD

What can you do when someone dies? Being that they are dead, you are very limited. But you will cremate, bury, entomb, or you may find them prepared and put on display as if there were life still in them. Yuk!

In August of 1995, Linda and I were living in Budapest, Hungary on a short-term project with Grace Ministries from Atlanta. From there I, and two fellow ministers had the opportunity to teach in a church planting school for Youth With A Mission (YWAM) in Krasnodar, Russia.

On the way home we had a one-day layover to spend in Moscow. We went with our Russian guides to Red Square to see some sites - the Kremlin, St. Basil's Cathedral, and Lenin's tomb.

Entering the dark tomb brought on an eerie pitch-blackness that contrasted the bright sunlit square. As we slowly descended the long stairwell, a faint light began to appear at the bottom right. My heart was feeling a bit weird as I knew I would come face to face with the body of an actual historical dictator who was (and is) much revered from the old Soviet Union.

As we entered the chamber, we made a U-turn to immediately go up another staircase. There he was! Lenin, lying under a glass shell. He looked as though he were napping and we were disturbing his sleep!

We came up the steps next to him passing first by his head on his right side. At the top of the stairs we turned to pass by his feet and then down the other side and made another U-turn that led to the exit stairwell. The chamber was fairly big and thankfully much cooler than the summer heat in Red Square.

It was so quiet in there. As I came up by his right side and onto the platform at his feet, I noticed that he had a deeply furrowed brow; a very hard look on his face. It was as though he would sit up any moment and make a speech. But on closer inspection, I noticed that Lenin appeared sort of wax-like. Yeah, like the wax figures in a wax museum. Say, was that really him? It was not easy to discern.

Upon our return to Budapest I discovered that Lenin's corpse is continuing to decay. Occasionally, the officials will close the tomb for repairs...on Lenin! Yes, part of what I saw was indeed wax. He looks lifelike, but there is no life. And all the fixing in the world will not stop the decay nor give him life. He is not just a little dead. He is radically dead. And has been!

I have seen many people who totally surrender themselves to God in order to be fixed. They truly see that they cannot fix fleshly decay in themselves and are even convicted that it is not possible. So, they turn themselves over to the only one who can - God. That may seem like a good idea, but having this as your goal in surrender can still leave you with a wrong focus. And a wrong focus will lead you to a dead end.

I've often heard it said that you can never become strong by focusing on your weakness. I find that those who continue to focus on the problem areas of their lives after surrender will not walk in the freedom that is theirs through Jesus Christ. They are, in effect, still trying to fix or wax the dead. They are waiting for the appearance of life where death reigned and are not experiencing actual life.

We do not experience freedom by continuing to focus on being fixed. This is focusing on death. God never intended for us to surrender in order for Him to repair the damage to our old man. Our "old man" was fit for one thing only - crucifixion!

For us to continue to look for changes in ourselves, after we have totally surrendered is only another form of bondage. This attitude does not make us available for Christ to live His life through us now, today. We are still waiting to live! We are telling God and ourselves that we cannot live until what's wrong in us is righted. And that is a lie.

What is God's solution to this? Simple...as it always is. He intended for you to embrace your death to the old you. It's dead. Get it? No life. But Satan wants you to believe that claiming your death, burial, and resurrection and surrendering totally to God means that God will fix what is wrong with you, and THEN you will be fine. Ney! Nein! Nyet! No way, man! Wrong answer! Not even close! Pick another card! As a new creation in Christ, you are made righteous with His righteousness and are equipped and ready to live right now; moment by moment with Christ as your life.

You see, focusing on what we want changed can never bring the freedom of life in Christ. Experiencing freedom from the old begins as we discover what is true about us in Christ. We embrace the death to the old, yes. But bury the thing! And don't continue to mourn the loss of your old ways to live. Don't go back and get all sentimental and put flowers on the grave and try to talk to it as if it were still alive. Bury the dead and go embrace the living. What does this mean?

To embrace the new man is to stand on the truth that God has made me complete, lacking nothing. There is nothing to fix or repair. As we focus on this truth, we will begin to experience the completeness of His life. We are free to begin to live in this moment. Yes, even with issues yet to be resolved you begin to "be who you are in Him". Resolving issues is His responsibility and He will get to them as He sees fit. (It probably won't be on your time table.)

What is victory? Well, for starters, that's the wrong question. Victory is not a "what". Victory is a "Who"! Who is Victory? Christ simply is Victory. We are full of Victory!

Are we still waiting for particular areas of our lives to be fixed in order to declare victory? Is our idea of victory that these areas have to change before we are OK? Aren't we already OK because we are in Him? OK = Righteous!

Christ wants us to know that we are OK in Him whether this area has changed yet or not. If we will embrace our death to the old man and embrace our birth to the new man, we will begin to experience His life being expressed in and through us more and more.

Well, what is victorious Christian living? Again, it is living with Christ as my life moment by moment. Not the events of victory yesterday nor the promise of victory tomorrow. Right now. This moment. Christ living His own life through me right now is victorious Christian living.

Waiting for life isn't living. You have life. His life. He's made you alive with His life. After having surrendered yourself into His hands and claiming your death in Christ, it is morbid to hang around the corpse of the old you. So, go out and live!

I was reminded recently that funerals are for the living. Have a funeral for the fleshly incapacitated old you. Don't stuff the corpse and then try to wax it up to look alive and healthy. It's dead and it stinketh!

Are you getting this yet? Don't focus on the dead hoping God will fix the damaged parts. It was only fit for crucifixion and burial. You have been created in righteousness and holiness of the truth. Walk in the light of who God now says you are and you simply won't be fulfilling the deeds of the flesh.

Moment by moment, trusting Christ as your life, walk out into life knowing that you are complete; growing into the expression of that completeness like an apple seed growing into the tree that it already is. When you are tempted to set your mind or eyes on what was wrong with the old man, respond saying something like the following:

"Wasn't it awful? Thank God the old me is dead and I don't have to try and fix it or ask God to fix it any more. That me is dead! Truly dead! Long live the new me! Righteous, redeemed, sanctified, glorified, complete me full of wisdom, grace and truth! Satan, if you want to put flowers on old me's grave, have at it. But I'm not going with you."

Focus on God and who He has made us in Christ. Find out from Scripture what is right with you. Stop going to the Word to just find out what is wrong with you. Focus on discovering what is right with you.

Set your mind on things above, not on things that are on the earth. For you have died and your life is hidden with Christ in God. Are there any dead things in Christ in God? Is there anything to be fixed or repaired in heaven? Then, don't focus on things crucified, buried on the earth. Repent of trying to fix yourself and waiting on God to fix you. Focus on your new identity in Him.

Dr. Peter Lord, one of my favorite preachers, and Robert McGee, author of *The Search For Significance*, taught me to confess the following:

"I am an awesome spirit being of magnificent worth as a person. I am deeply loved of God. I am fully pleasing to God. I am absolutely complete in Christ. When my person is expressed through my performance, the reflection is dynamically unique. There has never been another like me in the history of mankind, nor will there ever be. I am an original, one of a kind, really somebody, and so are you!"

If you began to treat yourself as who you already are instead of waiting for God to fix what you don't like about you, what do you think might happen? You might just begin to live! And live an abundant life at that! This is not denial that the flesh expression hasn't yet changed. It is putting off the old man and putting on the new man! Now look at this final illustration.

Let's say that your child had an old beat up tricycle that the wheels have fallen off, the handlebars are solid rust, the seat is broken and the frame is bent. What's it good for? Junk, right? You go buy your child a new one custom made just for them. You present it to your child and he or she says,

"Thank you! This is wonderful. Now if you'll just get this wheel back on here I can start thinking about riding again."

The child acknowledges the new but won't let go of trying to fix, give value to, and rescue the old. And they believe that they can't begin to think about riding again until they have satisfactorily repaired the old. What would you think? Why did you buy the new tricycle? You bought it in order that they could abandon the old and embrace the new. In your heart you could see the expressions of joy in their eyes as they whipped around in the driveway and down the sidewalk. But now you find them sitting in the back of the garage still in bondage to the old. Even though they know they can't repair it, they are bent on having you repair it before they can be OK and enjoy riding again.

Can you see how Satan has again tricked us? Sure we are convicted that we can't repair the old life from being in Adam. But do we truly realize that it is fit only to be crucified and buried? God is not interested in breathing His life into something destined for the grave. He has given us new life through the resurrection. Let us forsake the unrepaired, old, dead "us" and embrace and rest in the truth of the new "us" who is alive to God.

God wants you to get on your new tricycle and just ride! Remove your "value" from the old tricycle. Let Him bring you to see it as He sees it and let Him junk the old. And put on the new man, who in the likeness of God, has been created in righteousness and holiness of the truth.

So don't focus on the dead. Don't keep putting wax on it and stop expecting God to fix it. He's not interested. He has replaced the old with the new. Go discover and enjoy it!

9

FORGIVENESS RECEIVED

A thought came to me as I was teaching a class at church one Sunday concerning the story in Matthew 18 about the slave who had been forgiven an enormous debt yet had turned around and put one of his own slaves in prison for owing him a very small debt. I wish I could say that I understand and can explain that passage to its fullest, but I can't. There is more than one issue in this passage that is unclear to me, but I think God did show me something that I hadn't seen before.

The first slave benefited from the king's forgiveness, but did he really receive it? Here is why I ask: first, can you give something to another person that you haven't first received? The slave who was forgiven a large debt had only contempt for his own slave. Second, in the Gospel of Luke, Jesus says that one who is forgiven much, loves much and one who is forgiven little, loves little.

The first slave's plea was for a chance to repay the debt he owed to the king, it was not a plea for forgiveness. If he had received the gift of forgiveness it would stand to reason that he would then have had compassion and forgiveness for his own slave. Instead, he was bent on getting what he was owed in order to earn the gift he already had been given forgiveness.

Receiving forgiveness changes a person, whereas, repaying what you owe does not. Are we willing to admit that we were born sinners and were in need of much forgiveness? Have we really embraced the magnitude of how much we've been forgiven?

10

A
MUTANT GOSPEL

Christians sing a song of grace
That must have come from outer space.
It's all about the God of awe
And how we have Him under law
To give us all that we expect
Or we get mad and give Him heck!

Somehow we have crossed the two,
Grace and law, with mutant glue.
The monster that came to result
Is our image of God that we exult.
A God to be at our beck and call
But rarely seems to answer at all.

Our disappointment feeds our pain
Of being rejected again and again.
'Till grace from law is seen as pure
Our mutant image will endure.

Through Christ God gave us His Pure grace,
The law no more for righteousness!

No law on us, no law on Him
To make one perform at the other's whim.

We're free to love and be loved, too.
Free from bondage of mutant glue.
In Christ we died to law and sin.
His pure grace we now stand in.

If you want to know of what I speak,
There's nothing left for you to seek.
Surrender Him now your total will.
Your soul with grace and rest will fill.

11

LIVE

In 1999, while waiting on the arrival of Y2K, the year 2000, some people geared up for "the end." There was much talk about the possibility of major shutdowns and catastrophic events due to computers not being programmed to read a date that went beyond 1999. So much of our life is dependent on computers now: utilities, government agencies and businesses.

I heard a series of sermons during that time entitled "Living With The End In View". Catch what the title said? LIVING with the end in view. Not "Scared With the End in View" and not "Guarding My Stuff With the End in View." It said "Living."

We are still ambassadors of Christ's reconciliation, aren't we? And although I believe that the end will come, at the end of each day we are only one day closer. There is still plenty of ministry to do, plenty of life to live. Just remember to always keep the end in view because there will be an end. Live! Don't put off those things you wish you had done. Live! Don't put off mending those relationships that need to be mended. Live! Stay fluid with the Spirit within you to guide you effectively according to His purposes through your day. Live! Don't wait for some future event to take place before you can start to live. Live now! He has "made you alive with Him."

Romans 6: 8-11 says, *"Now if we have died with Christ, we believe that we shall also **live** with Him, knowing that Christ having been raised from the dead, is never to die again; death no longer is master over Him. For the death that He died, He died to sin, once for all; but the **life** that He **lives**, He **lives** to God. Even so consider yourselves to be dead to sin, but **alive** to God in Christ Jesus."* (Emphasis is mine)

Our burdens don't weigh more than a shadow to Him. Trust Him for NOW and live, in Christ, to life's fullest!

12

PARABLE OF THE TREES

I remember standing in my yard one summer afternoon and it occurred to me that I was observing a paradox. The trees, the yard and the street were soaked from another of several intense thunderstorms we had that year. Yet even with all of the rain, there in the heavily wooded yard stood four very dead trees. They were victims of the previous years of drought. It takes time for the effects of rainless summers to manifest in trees.

It rained so much that year you would have thought that one summer could make up for all of the previous waterless years. But the truth is that a flood of water one year is not able to overcome many years without steady consistent rainfall.

Galatians 6:8 says that the one who sows to his flesh shall from the flesh reap corruption. Romans 8:6 says that the mind set on the flesh is death. Colossians 3:25 says that we will receive the consequences, not punishment, of what we do without partiality.

The choices we make today set the course of events in motion that may take years to unfold. We may rationalize and say that the attitudes and actions we have long justified will have little or no effect on us or on others. We may still appear green, leafy, and full of life but underneath, the effects of barren times is working to undermine our lush exterior.

The marriage relationship may seem to go along with no apparent problems. The children appear to be in no visible rebellion. The business hasn't suffered any immediate setbacks. And then, seemingly without any notice, decay appears and accelerates rapidly.

All of our resources are trained to attack the decay, but it is too deep. Our frantic efforts are powerless. Even with all of our attention focused on battling the decay, death slowly but surely takes its victim; a leader falls, a marriage disintegrates, a virginity is lost, a friendship is damaged, or a child's respect has given way to rebellion. Control is lost to anxiety, depression, or outbursts of anger. But what seems to appear suddenly and seemingly without notice is in reality the surfacing of a problem that developed over a long period of time.

Some who are beginning to exhibit the inward decay may seek help while some may feel hopeless and helpless. Some simply want to be told what to do because as the pain surfaces, they want a "quick fix" that will lessen what they're feeling.

The truth is that people don't get into these messes in a day so it will take longer than a day to get out of the mess. Just as my yard can't recover from a decade of drought with one year of abundant rain, we can't immediately recover from years of bad choices by simply embracing Biblical truth. Even though some changes may be experienced right away, it can take months or sometimes years to heal the damage done.

Once we surrender to God and recognize our true identity in Christ as reality, we need to be content with being "in process." That means that we're not perfect, but we are growing at His pace in His grace, not escaping the present sufferings but being willing to let God use them to rid us of fleshly control so we can experience more of Christ's life within us.

Just as time and pressure turns a lump of coal into a diamond, God uses time and pressure to conform us to the image of Christ. Making choices based on our identity in Christ through day-to-day living will provide the basis to experience the recovery process. It takes time to replace old belief systems, heal emotions, and see a consistent walk in the face of recurring, conflicting feelings and circumstances. But restoration is available for those who seek Him.

13

TESTIMONY OF DEATH TO LIFE

March 15, 1981, was the day that my wife, Linda, and I discovered that we had died. Yep, you heard me right. It was the day we discovered our death and resurrection to new life in Christ. It was the day we discovered the practical reality of what our salvation in Christ meant for daily living and the day we began to understand our true identity in Christ. It was the day that would change our lives and our marriage forever. You may know our testimony but even so, you may not know some of the details I'm going to divulge here. This is a record of our journey. It is our thanks to God and it is our gift of hope to you.

Linda and I were married June 5, 1971, and we weren't that different from many who tie the knot. We had no clue what we were getting into and even on our wedding day I remember that I had to talk myself into going through with the ceremony. I had been taught that marriage was a lifetime commitment. But Linda was so good looking and she loved me as much as she or I could understand what that word meant.

I was a very controlling person, which came out even stronger once we were married. I now know that the degree that one controls is equal to the degree that person feels insecure, whether they realize that insecurity or not. Linda so wanted to please me that she went along with whatever I wanted for a long time. She wanted to prove that even though she was just 17, our marriage would not only work but also work well and be everlasting. The more she tried to fix the marriage and fix me the angrier I became. For a while, her fleshly coping mechanism of enabling fit very well with my fleshly need to control.

Over time, the very qualities that initially drew us to each other turned into the qualities that we disliked the most about each other. Eventually, Linda and I became distant, distrusting, and even hateful. The good times became the few and far between as the bad times grew plentiful. Regardless of what was really going on in our marriage, we were able to play the appearance game well. No one, including our pastor and our families, really knew what we were going through behind closed doors.

We were the youth directors at our church, taught Sunday school classes, sang in the choir and were part of a Christian music group that sang at churches, colleges and other public events. We never failed to be faithful, church-going servants trying to do what we thought we were supposed to do as Christians. But at home, the picture was quite different.

Our communication was a joke. We watched television while we played solitaire on opposite sides of the room. When we did speak to each other, it wasn't about our problems. We could only speak about our schedules and logistics of pulling off events. If we tried to talk about our problems we fought all the more. We reached unspeakable lows in our relationship with God, each other, and within ourselves.

When we were at the point of deciding which lawyer to use to put an end to our marriage, when all hope of a relationship was gone, when we were just coasting along in indifference to protect ourselves from more pain and pressure, God surprised us. It was March 1981, and we were miserable. For two weeks I had been praying, which looked more like I was reading God the riot act. I was telling Him off! I said, "I know I'm saved. I know I'm going to heaven. But what's with all this time in between? Why did You save me only to leave me here to wallow in all my failures? Why didn't You kill me when You saved me so I could avoid all this mess? I read Your Word, but I can't live what I see in Your Word. So, I quit! If You want it done, You're going to have to do it because I can't. And if You can't do it, then, I don't want to live anymore."

I hated God. I hated myself. I hated the mess I had made. I hated life. I wanted to die and relieve the pressure. Then I told God the words He had been waiting to hear, "Do with me whatever You choose." It was a total, absolute, and unconditional surrender. Little did I know that Linda had been praying an almost identical prayer. I poured my heart out to God for two solid weeks. All that time Linda and I were going through the motions in public of being the perfect little Christian couple. That facade was beginning to wear thin and the friction and tension that was present in our marriage were beginning to show through to those closest to us.

That is when God sent a friend to come and spend a weekend with us. God had been dramatically working in our friend's life and he was excited to get together with us and share what he had learned. To say we weren't up for company, especially overnight company would be an understatement. He was unaware of our struggle but his visit was definitely on God's time schedule. Our thought was that even if we didn't love each other, we still loved him and this might be the last time we saw him as a married couple.

Our friend was supposed to arrive on Friday night but ended up being delayed until Saturday morning. He came in around breakfast and, without knowing that we were in trouble, began unfolding the reality of our death, burial and resurrection with Christ. I found out that the "me" I hated had actually died on the cross in Christ and was buried with Him. Through His resurrection, I was given a brand new "me!" The "me" who was unable to live what I read in the Bible was dead. There was now a new "me," one that is with Christ and all that He is. (1 John 4: 17)

I found out that I am complete in Christ and no longer had to follow the intense urges of the flesh to defend myself against this world or fill myself with anything that the world had to offer me, including what I believed I needed from Linda in order for me to be okay. I learned that I was and am okay because I am in Christ. God says I'm okay and that truth set me free to stop focusing on what I thought I needed or desired and freed me to see myself and others the way our loving heavenly Father sees us. There is no other place to find this kind of peace that allows me to stand in the face of injustice and adversity, pain and sorrow. I am no longer a victim deceived. I am a victor set free.

Linda and I began to embrace the truth of God's Word from Romans 5, 6, 7 and 8, Galatians 2:20 and 21, 2 Corinthians 1:8-10, Colossians 2:9 and 10, 13 and 14. The Bible began to come to life! Our reactions to each other immediately began to change. When Linda did something that normally would have hurt me or made me angry, I knew I was safe and complete in Christ so I didn't have to react out of my feelings of emptiness like I had in the past. Instead, I could respond out of my fullness in Christ. (Ezekiel 36:26 and 27 and 1 Corinthians. 6:17) I didn't have to retaliate or be defensive. I didn't have to come back at Linda with curt verbal jabs and I didn't have to avoid her. I could risk a real relationship with her because I understood my true relationship to God. I was safe. No matter how deep of a wound or how intense the moment or how much my flesh wanted to react by defending or avenging, I was free from having to follow those fleshly ways!

I no longer had to live a life controlled by circumstances. No matter how bad or how good, no matter the past or the uncertainty of the future, I knew I could live in the moment with Christ as my life. That, my friend, is victory. That, my friend, is freedom. That, my friend, is the result of our old man's death on the cross in Christ and our resurrection to new life in Him. Salvation isn't just about gaining heaven and avoiding hell. Salvation is about a gift through Christ of death to my old life and inheritance in Adam. Salvation is also about gaining a totally new life and inheritance in Christ, a life that is available to us now on this planet in this existence! Heaven and eternity with God is a major bonus!

Wouldn't it have been cruel if He just saved us and made us suck it up and trudge around until physical death? Sadly, this is what many believe. They don't believe that there is an answer in their salvation through Christ to take them beyond where they are in their circumstances and suffering.

Before March 15, 1981, I used to ask God where was this abundant life He promised? There had to be more to Christianity than I knew or understood and at last I knew that was true! Knowing that I have been made righteous, complete and equipped for life here on Earth, knowing that I lack nothing pertaining to life and godliness, knowing that I am forgiven all my sins, knowing that I can't screw up enough that the Holy Spirit can't fix it if I'll let Him, lets me risk obeying God to the fullest. It lets me step out to try things I don't really feel equipped for, lets me rest when there is no rest and encourages me to stand firm when I am weak. It lets me be real when I feel scared or weak, lets me risk surrendering all results of my circumstances to God when my flesh is screaming at me to take control. Knowing who we are in Christ and what we possess because of our true identity in Him changes how we handle our lives now.

God is different than who we thought He was. He

is our all. Linda and I live more consistently out of truth than we do the lies programmed into us while children of Adam. Our faces are set like a flint on taking the Biblical truth that set us free to others who will listen. Life can be different and more full even if our circumstances never change. The abundant life promised in John 10:10 is not a life where all of my circumstances turn out the way I want or a place where I experience no pain and no suffering. The abundant life is freedom, it is peace and rest from being controlled by what my circumstances are or how they may or may not be resolved.

May God's blessings be multiplied to you as you seek His face.

Married June 5, 1971

Ray served in the
Naval Air Reserve
1971 - 1975

It all started when
Ray was a cadet at
North Georgia College
and stole my heart

Youth Ministry at
Westside Baptist Church,
Gainesville, GA 1977 - 1985

Counselor/Teacher
at Grace Ministries
International,
Marietta GA 1985 - 1995

Spent 1994 - 1995 counseling and teaching with Grace
Ministries in Budapest Hungary. WOW! What a year!

Counselor/Teacher and Director of Pastoral Support at Grace Ministries Inc., Manassas, VA 1996 - 2002

While living in VA we enjoyed being close to Washington D.C.

One of Ray's passions was teaching people the Truth from scripture.

Along with teaching he enjoyed other things as well.

Ray enjoyed traveling. He loved this picture in New York City 2000 because the Twin Towers were still in the skyline.

Ray was gifted artistically, and was not limited to pen and paper.

Music was a vital part of Ray's life. This was one of his favorite ways of expressing what was inside him.

Another thing that brought a smile to Ray's face was good food.

Ray loved to make people laugh and was good at it, whether he was playing a part in a skit at church, doing stand-up comedy,

"Polar Pete"

"Twas The Night Before Christmas", redneck version

or simply clowning around.

Christmas 2002

Ray Alton
January 19, 1950 - January 9, 2003

14

DISCOVERING THE GIFT

Some years ago, I labored under the pressure of trying to control an explosive rage. It was destroying my wife, my future, and me. I had no concept of God as being personal or loving. I actually felt God only tolerated me and that I was somehow a burden and disgrace to others and to Him. I felt that the standards were too high and that I didn't have what it took to live life, much less the Christian life.

My standards for my performance were actually higher than God's standards. I didn't know that He neither designed me nor did He expect me to perform perfectly. Perfection was and is the only standard acceptable to God and He let man struggle in his own strength to try and attain perfection. But God had a purpose. He wanted man to discover that he could never reach perfection through performance.

This is why Christ came. This is why He was broken and poured out at the cross for us. God wanted us to receive perfection, not achieve perfection. The perfection that is acceptable to God comes from God on the basis of faith—faith in Jesus Christ, the resurrected Son of the living God. Faith that says I believe that Jesus, through His relationship to the Father and Jesus' perfect obedience from birth to His death, burial, and resurrection, was enough to pay for all my sins and give me new life—His life.

Perfection is a gift. It is a gift from God and a gift of God to each person who simply claims Jesus as their Savior and Lord through faith. Perfection is a person not an excellent performance and it is His perfection, not what we can conjure up in our own strength to offer to Him that counts.

Another word for perfection is righteousness. If you are "right" with God, you are righteous. You receive His gift of righteousness by an act of faith. In this act you simply embrace for yourself the finished work of Jesus at the cross. Not just His death, burial, resurrection, and ascension into heaven and His being seated at God's right hand, but your death in Him, your burial in Him, your resurrection in Him, and your ascension and seating at God's right hand—in Him! Even when a child comes to God through faith in Jesus, perfection, righteousness, new life, and forgiveness of sins all become his or hers whether the child understands them all or not!

I remember one Christmas when I was invited to a party and I brought with me a present to be given in a gift exchange. Everyone put his or her gift in a pile and then we played a game of "Round Robin." The gift I brought was a set of nesting dolls from Russia. A man at the party chose my gift and he seemed to enjoy taking the dolls apart and discovering a smaller doll inside. But the man didn't open all of the dolls. Inside the last doll was a

$5 gift certificate for a local restaurant that I had folded into a tiny wad.

Here are some questions to consider. Even if the man at the party never discovered the gift certificate inside the last doll, wasn't it still his? Did the gift certificate loose its value or it's power to purchase because he had not experienced it? Did he have to understand the gift completely to receive it? Can we, then, receive Jesus Christ as our Savior and not totally understand the fullness of what that means?

As the man admired his gift, it was apparent that he was satisfied with what he knew about the gift. I wanted him to benefit fully from what I had given him so I went over and suggested that he open the last doll. To his amazement and joy he discovered the certificate! What a picture of how God works in us.

God offers gifts to us through Christ; a gift of total forgiveness, a gift of new life and a new identity, a gift of being made righteous, a gift of being made holy, and a gift of being made perfect forever in His eyes. We accept or reject these gifts by accepting or rejecting Christ. If we accept them, we only need a small understanding of their meaning to adequately claim them for ourselves. And, then, sometime afterwards, God begins to guide us to discover the depth of the gifts He has given to us. All of the understanding doesn't come at one time.

Some discoveries are easily done. It is evident that one treasure logically leads to another and another. But some gifts are not so easily tracked. You need guidance to go deeper. You may be content with the level of your discoveries in Christ but that doesn't mean that there isn't more you've yet to discover. That doesn't mean that someone else's deeper discovery is invalid for you and it doesn't mean that you are faulty. It does mean that God may disturb your contentment and beliefs and place you in pressure situations in order for you to discover more of the gifts of God through Christ.

I am thankful that many years ago God placed me in a desperate, desolate situation in order for me to open my heart and embrace my death, burial and resurrection in Christ. It was painful, but afterwards came peace and rest and discovery of what it means to have new life in Christ. Going deeper meant surrendering everything to Him, risking that He might bring things into my life that I desperately feared, or take things away that I held dear. It meant giving up all control over my life to Him. It meant trusting that He wouldn't take advantage of me.

God so much wants to show Himself to you in ways that, to this point, you have never before experienced. The prerequisite is embracing and receiving the gift as far as you can currently understand it. Each time you embrace a new discovery more will follow. If you resist, you limit yourself in discovering much of anything from God. Will you risk opening your heart to Him? Will you let Him reveal to you the riches He has laid up for you? Will you lay down all that is in your arms in order to receive the riches that He can't wait to give you?

PRAYER

Father, I am so tired of trying to control my life and my situations. I don't feel that You have been so much of a help either. I thought You wanted the things I wanted. They seem to be the right things as I read from scripture.

I don't know what Your plans are but I just can't keep going the way I'm going. I don't know if I can trust You, but I'm not getting anywhere by trusting in myself.

This article says that there is more to You than I have discovered. The implication seems to be that, if I surrender control completely to You, You will reveal more of Yourself in the midst of all the craziness of my circumstances. And further, that, I will somehow be better off than trying to control things myself.

My goal has been to change my circumstances. Your goal is to change me in my circumstances. I don't fully understand how that will make things better but I have nothing left to try on my own.

So, I surrender to You. I give total control to You for You to do whatever You wish with my circumstances and me. I give up my rights to understand what You're doing or why You're doing what You're doing. I give you permission to break me of trying in my own strength to handle this or any other situation to follow.

I now receive and claim that Jesus Christ is my Savior, Lord and Life. I receive all of the gifts from You that come in Him. I choose by an act of my will and embrace my death on Christ's cross. I have died in Him. I have died to having to be in control in order to be okay. In Him I am buried. The old me who needed control is dead and in the grave. In Him I am risen. I have a new life in Christ that is complete and doesn't need to be in control to be okay. Christ is what makes me okay, not being in control of my life. I am ascended and seated in

Christ. Being in Him I am already in heaven in Christ. I am victorious. What happens on this planet has no effect on my true place in Your heart and Your heaven.

Therefore, I am willing and choose to live within my present circumstances as long as You, God, see fit. I don't suggest that I understand all of it or even that I like being here but I am willing for You to accomplish Your perfect work in me through this mess. I trust that when it has worked its perfect work, You will remove the circumstances from me. I yield to Your timing and not mine.

In the meanwhile, I choose by faith and stand on Your truth that You are for me even if I can't see it now or if I never see it. Reveal to me, O Lord, all that You have given me in Christ that more than makes up for what I feel has been taken away.

In Jesus' name,
Your Child

15

WHAT AM I SAYING?

One Sunday as I was sitting in church listening to my pastor preach on Philippians 3:7-11, I found myself captured by verses 7 and 8, which says, *But whatever things were gain to me, those things I have counted as loss for the sake of Christ. More than that, I count all things to be loss in view of the surpassing value of knowing Christ Jesus my Lord, for whom I have suffered the loss of all things, and count them but rubbish in order that I may gain Christ.*

I meet so many people who, when confronted with surrendering their dreams, fears, expectations, rights, reputations, welfare of their children, marriages, houses, jobs, financial situations, and anything else that needs to be surrendered, they will come back at me with, "I know that I need to surrender this, but I am just not ready." Underneath that statement is the following thinking. "I want more proof that God will lean more toward providing me with what I want. What they are saying is that they are unwilling to give up possession or the illusion of control of all things. Let's reword the above verses to reflect the real belief, the belief that may not be so easy to see.

"Whatever things were gain to me, those things I have counted more valuable than Christ. More than that, I count all things as surpassing the value of knowing Christ Jesus as my Lord, for whom I am unwilling to suffer the loss of all things and unwilling to count them as rubbish to just gain Christ." FV (Flesh Version)

Examine your heart in light of the flesh version. Is this what you really believe? Is this what your present stand and actions say? You are standing in the face of making a decision about absolute surrender to God. You will actually be choosing one or the other of these versions of belief and action, either the Biblical version or the flesh version. Whatever you choose, you will reap the consequences of that belief and that choice. Which way will you choose to go? Will you retain control of all things or surrender them to Him?

16

HOBO AND BARNEY

Do you ever wonder why God is reported to be so interested in man? Maybe you know the answer or maybe you've never pondered this question. Maybe you don't care because you don't really think there is a God or, if there is, He hasn't seemed all that interested in your affairs in a visible way. Okay. But on the chance that you just became interested, I have a few thoughts for you to consider. Let me tell you two stories.

Years ago my wife, Linda, and I were given a puppy. We had just lost a precious pet to a road accident and weren't exactly in the market for another one. In fact, we were emotionally drained over losing this particular dog.

At that time I worked for a man whose wife volunteered at a local animal hospital. She had found a bedraggled, hungry, little puppy near a dumpster. She took it to her vet and was preparing it to be adopted when she got the news that we had lost our dog. One day while I was working my boss came in with something under his arm. My first thought was that I couldn't afford to love another animal that soon. It was so painful to lose Scruffy that I just didn't want to even look at this little orphan. I couldn't bear the possibility of loving another dog to maturity and then losing it too.

Then my boss said, "This little dog needs loving, too." That did it. I took her home. She slept in a box next to the bed until she became secure and used to us. We named her Hobo, reflecting the circumstances under which she was found. And we loved her. But she was very different from Scruffy. She was a yard dog, not a house dog. She stayed mostly in our fenced-in backyard. She wanted nothing to do with cuddling or being still. She was a small, black and tan, four-legged, wiggling, fur covered muscle with big eyes and an appetite!

During the time we had Hobo, we moved from our hometown. As we searched for a house, we kept in mind that this house would also have to work for Hobo. There would need to be an area suitable for fencing-in a rambunctious 13-pound terrier whose whole body wagged in rhythm with her tail. Part of our decision on a house actually depended on the value we had set on this dog.

When she reached the age of 15, she was in bad shape. She was nearly deaf and blind, couldn't smell, and walked on three legs. She would snap at you when you touched her because she couldn't tell what or who you were. To the world she was worthless. She had nothing to give. She required so much effort and so many resources yet she could give us nothing in return. But it didn't matter. You see, we didn't love and value Hobo because of who she was. We loved and valued Hobo because of who we are. We loved her because we chose to love her. Our love for her was not controlled by how great a dog she could be. She didn't do tricks. She couldn't cuddle and she would scare the neighborhood with a forlorn, lonely, blood-curdling howl that constantly put us in a position to have to explain. The neighbors thought we were beating her until they got to know her habits! Hobo could do nothing for us in order to earn our love. We simply chose to love, value, and care for her until she passed away from natural causes. I still miss her at times.

Do you see it? Why would God be interested in you or me for that matter? It has nothing to do with who we are. We have nothing to trade the Creator of the universe for His interest in and love and value for us. That's just who He is. He is love and He loves us out of who He is. What about His wrath on sinners? I don't know what you've heard, but hear me out for a minute. God is righteous, holy, perfect, and cannot tolerate sin. Does that match what you've heard about Him so far?

God couldn't just overlook sin and freely love us at the same time, so before He made the world He came up with a plan. He would have a Son, send Him to earth and this Son would be the perfect sacrifice for man's sin and sinfulness, for all men for all time. Quite a plan, huh? So this Savior, this Messiah, was birthed in human form, a baby boy who was named Jesus, which means, "God with us." The Bible says that in the fullness of time, Jesus, the Christ, the Savior, died for the ungodly - for you and me and the rest of man.

Some people teach that Jesus died on that cross to pay a ransom to Satan to set us free in order that we could go to heaven some day. Not true. There was no ransom due Satan. The problem God had was with Himself. He is

Righteous Judge and He is Love but how can He love if His judgment would destroy us? The answer is: Jesus' sacrifice met God's demand for payment for sins. His righteous judgment had to be satisfied and Jesus did that on our behalf, completely taking it out of the way so God's love can be expressed unhindered. If we will personally accept Jesus' payment for our sins and our sinfulness, our hearts are then open to experience God's expressions of love.

Oh, the other story. I have a brother in Christ named Barney. Barney is a card-carrying physician, psychiatrist, and full-time missionary to missionaries. He travels the world over giving aid of all kinds to missionaries who take the message of salvation by faith to the nations. Barney, his wife, and one of their daughters made a journey to India to minister at an orphanage. His wife is a nurse and his daughter just loves children.

When they arrived, Barney tried to fit his talent, training, and giftedness into the circumstances found at the orphanage. Much to Barney's dismay, the orphanage didn't need his expertise in any area he had prepared to offer them. The staff and children needed the talent, training, and giftedness of his wife and daughter but poor Barney, who admittedly thrived on earning attention from others, couldn't do, fix or improve a thing for these people. But the children came up to him constantly, loving on him daily.

Barney became more and more uncomfortable because the attention and love he was receiving was unearned. He didn't feel worthy because he had not done anything to deserve such an outpouring of love from the children. He found himself frustrated and agitated and then he finally understood. He saw what he could not see beforehand. These children didn't love him because of his great doctoring ability or his great missionary training or his understanding of man's mind and emotions. They didn't love him for his wonderful sense of humor because they couldn't even understand him. They didn't love him because of who he was. They loved him because of who they were. They just simply loved him.

Barney didn't ask for their love apart from his performing something for them but they loved him regardless of his performance. He became the object of the expression of love that was already in them to give. In learning why they loved him, he learned the depth of God's love for him apart from his ability to earn it.

God loves you. God wants you. Barney finally let go and received the love of these children and also God's love for him. Will you let go and receive God's love for you? Are you fearful of failing at Christianity? The good news is that it is not a contest. He simply offers through Christ a new life, His life in you. He will walk you through all that you don't understand. We can't live a Christian life in our own strength, but with Christ in us, He can, when we let Him.

Are the actions and attitudes of others, who claim to be religious, making Christianity look like a farce? Listen, this isn't about religion with its list of do's and don'ts. It's about a relationship with the God who made you. A lot of folks don't really understand this and are striving to gain something they already have, His love and acceptance. Does this make sense to you?

Will you let go of trying to improve your self-image and your sense of self-worth? You can never by your performance earn enough points to overcome being born spiritually sinful. Our very best will never be enough to gain His life or heaven. Will you simply by faith receive to yourself the undeserved, unearnable gift of salvation from God through Jesus Christ?

17

LESSONS LEARNED FROM BURNOUT

Have you ever experienced burnout? I know I have, and it's not fun. However, I can say that I'm thankful for what I experienced because I came out the other side of burnout having learned some very valuable lessons. I hope the things I've learned will help you too:

1. I can't do it all and I'm not supposed to do it all. God never designed me to do it all.
2. I can't please everyone and that's okay. I really won't die and neither will they if I don't please them the way they want me to or think I should.
3. I am not responsible for anyone's happiness. I don't have to make them happy in order for me to be okay. Christ alone is what makes me okay. I am responsible to God for each of my relationships.
4. Practice saying "No" to something today.
5. I don't owe anyone an excuse or reason for doing

or not doing something. I am free to offer one, but I don't owe one.

6. I have all the time I need to accomplish everything that God wants me to do today.

7. I am no one's last hope! I am not the Messiah. Jesus is our only hope.

8. I do not have all the answers and that's okay.

9. Just because I can do it or because I enjoy doing it, doesn't mean that I'm supposed to do it. (Serving man vs. serving God)

10. I will not compare myself to others or to their positions, talents, relationships, abilities, spirituality or possessions. I am complete in Christ. I lack nothing. (Colossians. 2:9, 10; II Peter 1:3)

11. I can risk standing alone and not be controlled by the demands or expectations of others.

12. I have struggles too, and that's okay.

18

CRUCIFIED TO NEW LIFE

Adversity came, no break was in sight.
The waves were unceasing, how long could I fight?
As I sank exhausted, still struggling for air,
I accepted my death with fears all a glare.

To my surprise, in death there was found
Peace and protection, inside, all around.
For as I received the death that was mine,
True life was discovered when before I was blind.

My strength in the way only brought on more pain.
Accepting my death is God's way to life's gain.

Before when I struggled to live life my way,
I carried my burdens in misery each day.
Accepting my death, passing through to New Life,
The burdens fell off, thus ending my strife.

Resting in Jesus, His death being mine,
His life now takes care of the burdens unkind.
By faith as I rest, safe and secure,
Emotions will settle in time, I am sure.

But each time I act and forget I have died,
I remember how useless my strength when I tried.

By faith I choose constant that position of rest,
For it's His life in me that accomplishes best.
I'm now more at ease with this new life I own.
Though the emotions remain the old life is gone!

I praise you, O Father, for the freedom I know.
Belief systems changing as onward I go.
Deeper in rest, as troubles roar o'er,
Established in Christ, perfected the more.

19

ENOUGH, COMPLETE, AVAILABLE

Is the pace at which you do the work of God killing the work of God in you? What do you do when you begin to realize that you are no longer soaring but flapping like crazy to maintain momentum and motivation? God has deeply impressed three words on me that will be the cornerstone of my current ministry and any future ministry. The three words are *Enough, Complete,* and *Available.*

Several years ago when I was being extremely fractious and argumentative with my wife, she sent me on a personal retreat. She needed a break and I needed to figure out and deal with whatever was eating on me. I gathered my Bible, several devotionals, a couple of books that had spoken to me in the past, a pen, paper, boom box and praise music, some Oreos and Slim Fast and went to a hotel and locked myself in for a couple of days.

During the first day and into that evening I poured my heart out to God in anger, frustration, and tears. I threw all the dissatisfaction and disappointment I was feeling about how I thought my life was progressing and the sorry prospects I saw for the future at Him. I lamented my perception of His lack of involvement and support for the ministry to which He had called me. Later I read, played music and just listened. I was determined that I wasn't leaving there until I heard from God, or at least that was the plan.

As my soul quieted from having poured out all the poison within me, God began to show me in Scripture, devotions, and music that He is *enough* for me. Nothing else needs to be gained. Nothing else needs to change. Nothing else needs to happen or resolve. Nothing in the future is so great or painful that God alone won't be enough. The Spirit of the living "I AM" lives in me. He is enough for me to not be controlled by what has happened, what is happening, and what might happen. I began to rest again as I realized that He truly is enough. Years ago I heard someone ask, "Why is it that we will trust God for the rest of eternity, but we won't trust Him for the next fifty to sixty years?" Is He enough or do we look to another?

The next word God focused on is the word *complete*. You and I have been made complete in Him. This is something that I have majored on in ministry for many years. One of the greatest weaknesses of Christians is that we don't know who we are in Christ and what we have because of who we are. Satan wants you and me to believe that we are not complete and not all that we say we are. Then he baits us to try and prove through our flesh that we are who we say we are. Or Satan gets you to bail out of the game, pull up the covers, and become functionless for the cause.

Even Satan's attacks on Jesus, recorded in Luke 4:1-13 and 23:35-39 challenged Him to defend who He was and what He possessed. If You are who You say You are, prove it by meeting your needs, and if You have the power You say You do, prove it by testing it by saving Yourself. If Satan used these tactics on Jesus Himself, why do we think he would do any less with us? Satan uses even God's law to beat us half to death so we are rendered powerless for the purpose of reconciling others to Him.

In Colossians 2:9-10, God says that through Christ you and I have been made complete. If I embrace that belief, Satan has nothing to sell me. 2 Peter 1:3 says I have been granted everything I need. Ephesians 1:3 says I am fully blessed. I don't have to wait until the future to start living. I can live right now while God is delivering me from putting faith in my old fleshly ways of meeting my perceived needs or protecting those things that I have tried to draw life from other than Christ.

The third word I heard was *available*. I did a word study on the word "alive" as it is used in Scripture. I wanted to know what it meant to be "alive to God." It finally came to me that the practical application of that phrase is "available." I am fully connected to God and available for His life to flow through me into this world. It's like a coffee pot, plugged in and ready for use. Whether it is being used at the moment or not, it is available.

I read a story years ago written by Rev. Ron Dunn about a little kitchen faucet. The owner of the house walked into the kitchen and found the little faucet sad and he asked him what was wrong. The little faucet said, "I feel so bad because I haven't done anything for you today. I haven't washed your hands, poured you water, or anything and I feel so useless and worthless."

The owner said, "Oh, little faucet, don't you know that you don't have to do anything to bring me pleasure? The thing that gives me great pleasure is to come in here and find you available any time I need you. And, by the way, you cannot turn yourself on. It is I who turns you on to dispense water for my purposes." [1]

As I thought about this story, it grew in my head to include all the spigots, faucets, and other water valves in and outside my house. They were all hooked together by pipes so they could talk to each other. I imagined them talking about their positions in the household and their value to me, their owner.

The one in the kitchen was bragging about how often and all the different ways he was being used. The one in the shower was just as proud because he was used everyday. The one attached to the icemaker was excited because even though no one could see him, he was working all the time. Even the toilets were talking about how they served a valuable service. The little spigot behind the holly bush on the front of the house was crying because he was hardly ever used. He wasn't even used to wash the cars. His only function was to water the lawn when the ground got too dry.

As the owner of all the spigots, I would love to say to that little one behind the holly bush, "Little faucet, don't you know that you bring me great pleasure simply because you are there and available? Did you know that if you weren't here, I would have to run a hose all the way from back of the house? And did you know that I cut the holly bush away from you just so I could reach in to where you are to turn you on? It isn't how much you are used that pleases me, it's the fact that you are always ready and available to me."

God is enough. I am made complete in Him. When I make myself available to Him, He will express His enoughness through my completeness in this moment. That, my friends, is victory. Victory is Christ living His life, which is enough and makes me complete, in and through me in this moment. The last moment is gone and the next is not promised. This is the only moment we have to experience Christ as our life, living through us, through our unique personalities and releasing us to be all that He created us to be in Him.

This reality has gotten me through many tough spots of waiting on God's timetable, failures on my part, failures on the part of others, uncertainties, pains, pressures, as well as coming down from a huge success before pride or fleshly self-confidence sets in.

Let me say this one more time. God is enough. I am made complete in Him. When I make myself available, He will express His enoughness through my completeness in this moment. That, my friend, is victory!

20

SUFFERING: A GOOD AND PERFECT GIFT?

All good and perfect gifts come from God. However, what about those situations handed to us that are much less than pleasant? From where do they come? Do these come from Satan or could they also come from God? And if they come from God, what happened to the "good" and "perfect" description of God's gifts?

The Apostle Paul tells us in Philippians 4:6 and 1 Thessalonians 5:18 to give thanks in everything. Some have had the idea that God is not in control of the initiation of suffering which comes to us, but will control the resolve on our behalf if we do our part of giving thanks.

Consider Ephesians 5:20 - *always giving thanks for all things in the name of our Lord Jesus Christ to God, even the Father.* Here we see that since we are instructed to thank Him for all things, then He is much more involved in what gets through to us. Whatever gets through to us has to go through God and through Jesus first, then whatever it is finds us full of Jesus who is there to handle the problem on our behalf. John 14:20 says, *In that day you shall know that I am in My Father, and you in Me, and I in you.*

Romans 8:20 and 21 says, *For the creation was subjected to futility, not of its own will, but because of Him who subjected it, in hope that the creation itself also will be set free from its slavery to corruption into the freedom of the glory of the children of God.*

Give this some thought. We are God's creation. In order to set us free from our slavery to corruption by subjecting us to futility, would God offer to us a good and perfect gift of suffering?

21

TWO THOUGHTS TO PONDER

Do you have simple faith? Many times we let man's wisdom complicate or destroy our faith. Recently I heard two statements that deeply impressed me and I hope they might impress you too.

On a pastors' retreat that I attended, some men got unexpectedly honest and vulnerable about personal hurts they had experienced admitting that they did not know how to overcome them. I listened with great interest as they admitted their inability to handle these situations. One man who had experienced one of the deepest hurts provided us with a most profound thought.

Out of his pain he had sought God with all his heart. Day after day, week after week, year after year he prayed and received no discernible answer. He said that he was left with one course of action. He said, "When there was no reply from heaven after many seasons of prayer and tears, I threw myself upon the silence of God."

Only there did he find the peace and rest to move on with the rest of his life and ministry. Are you facing something where you have prayed and prayed and it seems as if God hasn't heard you? Be assured that he has heard and now, by simple faith, throw yourself upon the silence of God and discover His peace. Many situations have no resolve, but God is still there for you.

The second thought to ponder concerns our desire to do things right for the Lord. We really do desire to perform well, but we don't always reach our desired standard. A choir had put in hours and hours of practice and all were aware that the whole Easter pageant could be better. But one man of simple faith was asked to pray before the actual performance and this is what he prayed, "Lord, we may not get it right tonight, but You did." What matters? How well we perform or how well He performed? What secures our salvation, our performance or His?

22

WALK
IN TRUTH

Help! The snow has fallen and I can't get out! I remember one particular winter while living in Virginia that made up for the previous mild winters in spades! We had three significant snowfalls in as many weeks. That's probably not much to some of you but for this Georgia boy it was a lot. Actually, harsh or mild, I'm glad there are seasons and I am glad there are seasons to our spiritual growth as well.

Many years ago I experienced a major season of growth followed by a long season of bone-dry existence. I prayed and studied and fretted over why it seemed that the windows and doors of heaven had shut and why I wasn't getting any new illumination. One night God answered that question in my thoughts. It sounded like this: "Son, if I showed you all of my light at once, you couldn't take it. You would reduce to a cinder. So, I show you some truth and then give you a season to walk in it before I show you more."

Wow! I had felt that God had removed Himself from me but it wasn't true. He was proving His faithfulness to me as I put in practice the things He had already shown me. He wanted me to experience the truth I knew before putting more on my plate. Could He be doing that with you? Are you going through what seems to be a dry season with Him? What was the last thing He showed you? Are you taking the opportunities to walk in that truth?

What I'm saying is, it's not a good idea to expect Him to give you more knowledge until you're willing to walk in what He's already shown you.

23

REMIND ME

God, help me be real, even if it's "real" bad. If I need to see my flesh, reveal it to me, no matter how ugly it may be. If I need to see how much You love me, show me, no matter how much I may shy away because of my feelings of inadequacy or worthlessness. Because of indwelling sin, I am constantly tempted and will sometimes forget what I know to be true; that indwelling sin and my flesh are not me, though I still have responsibility to deny it access through my soul; that I am crucified, buried and raised with Christ, exchanged at the cross from death as Adam's sinful offspring to birth as God's righteous child.

Remind me that I don't have to be anything or anyone different than who You created me to be. And, please, remind me often that others don't have to become different than who they are in order for me to be complete. You have made me complete in Christ.

Remind me that I am truly a new and whole person through Christ.

Remind me that not even You have to change or do anything else in or around me for me to be okay. You simply are what makes me okay in each moment.

Remind me to rest in You when I am tempted to

become anxious over interruptions, injustices, deadlines, obstacles, potential pain, and especially the consequences of my own failures.

Remind me that You are Sovereign over all of these issues.

Remind me that through Christ You have settled all my failures.

Remind me that You can weave even the most stupid act into the tapestry of "all things" working together for good. (Romans 8:28)

Remind me that when I experience no rest, You are my Rest. When there is no strength, You are my Strength. When there is no joy, You are my Joy. When there is no peace, You are my Peace. You are the great "I am" (whatever I need) every moment I breathe.

Remind me that I am never alone. As Al Holley wrote in his song "You are nearer to me than my hands and my feet; closer to me than my breath." [1]

24

WHAT'S MISSING?

In the spring of 1995, it came to my attention that I had been in bondage to a lie of Satan. This lie is so subtle, yet so strong, that I find it close to or at the bottom of most problems that hound others too. The lie is the fear of missing out. Do you think that's too simple? That is precisely what Satan is counting on, that it is too simple to actually be the answer to a long and heavy bondage.

The truth is that we fear missing out on something that we, at gut-level, believe we must have in order to be complete in that moment, that day, that week or that year. We believe we are incomplete and that we must have achievement, recognition, a possession, a person, an emotion, or an attitude that we fear could get by us in order for us to be complete. Let's look at the truth and then come back to some examples of the lie and how we could apply the truth in a practical way.

Colossians 2:9 and 10 says that I am made complete in Christ. Complete! Not lacking! No holes! No pieces missing! *For in Him all the fullness of Deity dwells in bodily form, and in Him you have been made complete, and He is the head over all rule and authority...*

II Peter 1:3 says that I have been divinely granted through His power everything pertaining to life and godliness. *Seeing that His divine power has granted to us everything pertaining to life and godliness, through the true knowledge of Him who called us by His own glory and excellence.*

I John 4:17 says that as He is, so also am I in this world....now! *By this, love is perfected with us, that we may have confidence in the day of judgment; because as He is, so also are we in this world.* He is the fruit of the Spirit. I have all the peace I need, all the patience I need, all the love I need, all the joy I need, all the goodness I need, all the gentleness I need, all the self-control I need, all the faithfulness I need, and all the meekness I need. Everything I need I have because I have Christ as my life.

In Ephesians 2:4-6 and Colossians 3:1-3 it is clear that I am already in heaven in Christ. *But God, being rich in mercy, because of His great love with which he loved us, even when we were dead in our transgressions, made us alive together with Christ (by grace we have been saved), and raised us up with Him, and seated us with Him in the heavenly places, in Christ Jesus, — If then you have been raised up with Christ, keep seeking the things above where Christ is, seated at the right hand of God. Set your mind on the things above, not on the things that are on earth. For you have died and your life is hidden with Christ in God.*

Are people in heaven missing anything? Do people who are already in heaven have all the righteousness they need? All of God's acceptance they need? All God's love they need? All the worth or value they need? If Christ's life is my life through His death, burial, and resurrection with simple faith receiving Him to myself, haven't I had a life transplant? And all which is true about Christ is true about me. As He is, so am I. Does this sound like a needy person? Does this sound like someone who has "missed it" or "missed out?" If you have received Christ as your Savior, you are no longer needy and missing anything. God is everything! Jesus Christ lives inside you! God is the great "I AM." I AM whatever you need, whenever you need it!

In 1995 I was "stuck" in bondage to an old flesh pattern. The pattern was degrading to me and it finally came to the surface with a friend. This friend told me that I was believing the lie that in order to be free, I had to discover some "missing key" and unless I found that key I couldn't be free. Then he said, "And the missing key is that there is no missing key." It was true! I was walking in freedom in several other areas but I believed that I must be missing something or I wouldn't be continuing in this particular fleshly bondage. When I saw the lie, the hold was broken and I have walked in freedom from that day.

Satan tempts us with the underlying message that if we don't snap up what he offers then we have missed what we need. For example, take a man who is in bondage to lust and put him in a restaurant. He sees a beautiful girl dressed in a sensual manner. Satan wants him to stare at her and wallow in fantasies that do not line up with who he is in Christ. How does Satan get him to lock in to the fantasies? He sets him up in some other area of his life.

The messages may center around missing out on being a real man. Circumstances at work or at home that attack his worth leave him believing that he is wanton and needy, that he is missing out on the good things in life like being in the arms of this woman in the restaurant. Because he believes he is missing out, he is set up for a stronger emotional response to the stimulus in front of him. If this man is put down at work or at home or even grew up in a home where he was put down, what would lusting after this woman do for him? What is he missing that a fantasy with her could complete? How important does this man believe he is? How loved? How significant? How desirable as a man? How much power does he believe he has? How acceptable does he believe he is?

What can he be, feel, and do in a fantasy? Anything his heart desires. If he needs to feel powerful, then he'll fantasize about her falling under the spell of his fantasized manliness. Does he need to feel important or loved or accepted? In a fantasy he can be anything, have anything, and control anything he believes will complete him. Satan will deceive you into believing that you are missing something that you are supposed to have in order to be complete. Think how advertisements are set up.

"Don't miss this opportunity for savings..."
"Why should you be the only one in the neighbor-hood without a new..."
"This sale will be for one day only! Don't miss..."
"Don't miss this once-in-a-lifetime concert!.."

Most things advertised to us are not needs but a way to get our perceived needs met. If I am told that I will have more value by wearing a toupee or have hair transplants, I am getting two messages. The first is that I currently am less valuable, less important, less acceptable, and less loveable than someone who has a full head of hair. The second message is that I must have this product to become what I think I'm missing. This thing, or the lack of this thing then becomes the generating powerhouse that controls my way of getting this hair that I'm lacking! I become consumed by "getting me some hair!"

Then, you get you some hair only now you find out that you don't have the right look. Now you go out and get fitted from head to toe with a new look only to find out that you don't have the right car only to find out that you don't have the right job to make the right money to buy the right car and...puff, puff, puff,...whew!

Look at all this stuff! And it's never enough! There's always more stuff to have to be, to have, or to do! Always chasing after that one-more-thing that will make you complete! I know this all sounds weird and I'm not trying to poke fun at anyone. Satan does that enough. He wants you to chase your tail about whatever he can get you to believe you don't have enough of. Is it your dad's love? You'll chase him for it or believe that you'll never be okay because you'll believe that because it's missing from your life that you can never be complete. Is it sexual affections from your mate? You'll drive your mate away trying to complete yourself through them. Your mate is not God. But you make them your god by saying that they have to do something to complete you.

Can you see how we are using and abusing many "desire" categories to meet our deep needs. Can you see that your drive to get these categories is driven by a belief that you are not complete? Can you see that Satan has lied to you about your completeness and about who God really is? Does Satan want you to ever find out that you are made complete in Christ? No! Would he, then, try to conceal and twist truths in order to keep you from ever wanting to find out the truth? Would he tell you that the truth is too simple and that there is no practical application from the truth to your situation? Absolutely!

What is the truth? Man was created in the image of God but traded that image for the belief that he was missing something, specifically wisdom. He got that belief by reasoning with Satan. Adam already had wisdom because he had God but through his act of disobedience he lost for all of us the worth God had placed on us. Through Christ, God restores all of this completeness upon our act of faith, believing and confessing that Christ Jesus is our Savior and Lord. In II Peter 1:3 it says that God calls us through His OWN glory and excellence...not ours. Ephesians 4:23 and 24 says, ...*and that you be renewed in the spirit of your mind, and put on the new self, which in the likeness of God has been created in righteousness and holiness of the truth.*

When you find yourself passionately pursuing something or someone, ask yourself this question. Am I trying to complete myself? What will gaining this do for me? What deep need am I trying to get met by this thing or this person I'm pursuing? The truth is that our needs have already been met in Christ so I can walk away without getting whatever it is I've been pursuing. I won't die without it. You've already died in Christ and come alive to God through Christ with a new life and have all of your needs for love, acceptance, righteousness, security, and value met in Him. I don't have to control anything or anyone in order to be complete.

You might ask, "What about those we love who die and leave us behind to mourn and miss them?" You may feel that your loved one was "taken from you." My dad has been dead for several years and I miss him now as much as I ever have. But my dad doesn't complete me. He doesn't have to be here in order for me to be complete, right, or perfect.

What about a woman who has had an abortion, who realizes that she "missed" the opportunity to know and love that child and be loved by that child? Having or losing this or any other opportunity does not complete a person. Only God through Christ completes a person.

This is freedom. My mistakes and the mistakes others have done against me do not have to be undone or erased from history for me to be complete. The death, burial, and resurrection of Christ makes me complete and what I appropriate from God on the basis of faith sets me free! And there is total forgiveness for my sinful mistakes and other's sinful mistakes against me!

When you stand on the truth that you are already complete in Christ, then you can begin to see the lie of Satan that has kept you stuck or paralyzed. Be free because you are free! Galatians 5:1 says, *It was for freedom that Christ set us free; therefore keep standing firm and do not be subject again to a yoke of slavery.*

You are complete in Him! You are missing nothing! He will teach you all things and guide you to all things. As the lies are revealed, let His completeness fill up even those places where you feel your emotions are lacking. You have great worth because He gave you great worth through Jesus Christ our Savior, Lord, and Life!

25

SO, YOU WANNA BE BOSS

Has it ever occurred to you that God never struggles to figure out the best way to handle a problem? When God thinks, He is not thinking in order to solve a problem. When He thinks, He is expressing Himself and if He speaks, He speaks the thought into being. You and I will never face a problem that will set God on edge with anxiety as to how to resolve it and nothing can ever catch God by surprise. Whether it is a failed marriage, a financial crisis, an injury, an illness, or even a death, there is no problem that can so concern God as to get Him out of His chair to pace the floor with worry.

God is sovereign. God is omniscient. He knows everything from eternity past to eternity future. Nothing can get by Him without His notice. Nothing can get by without His allowing grace and power. In fact, God causes well-being and creates calamity. He forms light and creates darkness. Could this be possible? *That men may know from the rising to the setting of the sun that there is no one besides Me. I am the LORD, and there is no other, the One forming light and creating darkness, Causing well-being and creating calamity; I am the LORD who does all these.* Isaiah 45:6 and 7

Think about it. Could Satan exist if God didn't create him? Could Satan have power that God didn't give him? Could Satan remain the ruler of this world, the prince of the power of the air, if God didn't allow it? When something bad happens to us, why are we so quick to ask why? Why ask why when it isn't even about life in THIS life? God didn't create us in order that we should come up with and implement solutions to the problems in this life. This life isn't simply about crisis management. He said in Romans 8:28, *ALL things work together for good...* didn't He? Then, there must be more to life than we've understood.

Could God be responsible for even all of the yukky stuff in my life? I don't even ask those kinds of questions any more. Life isn't about events and their origin or their resolve. Life is about a true and vital relationship with THE Creator of all things. God isn't as concerned with what problem you have as much as He is in whom you are depending on to face the problem. Is there any problem too hard for God? Then what difference would it make what problem you have? All problems, then, are important to God and they are all important for the same reason: Finding His life through Christ Jesus from which to respond to any problem. *I have been crucified with Christ; and it is no longer I who live, but Christ lives in me; and the life which I now live in the flesh I live by faith in the Son of God, who loved me, and gave Himself up for me.* Galatians 2:20

But we have this treasure in earthen vessels, that the surpassing greatness of the power may be of God and not from ourselves; we are afflicted in every way, but not crushed; perplexed, but not despairing; persecuted, but not forsaken; struck down, but not destroyed; always carrying about in the body the dying of Jesus, that the life of Jesus also may be manifested in our body. For we who live are constantly being delivered over to death for Jesus' sake that the life of Jesus also may be manifested in our mortal flesh. II Corinthians. 4:7-11

Some of us are great at throwing pity parties and depression drunks and anxiety brunches and panicked fear-of-the-future orgies. So, when these are your experience, whose abilities and strength are you trusting in order to face the problem? Yours? You control this? For how long? What happened the last time you controlled the problem? Did it stop the problem? Were there more problems to follow? How long can you keep this up? What if you expend all your strength and the problem doesn't go away, what do you do then? Are you still the best person on whom to rely?

On whom, beside yourself, have you depended? Are they available for each and every problem? What happens when they aren't around? Who do you go to then? Can you honestly say that you want to spend the rest of your life as your own defense, your own security, or your own meeter of your needs? Who does this super-human description sound like to you? Maybe God?

There is a God and you're not Him. Because of our perception of the feedback during our lives we have a skewed concept of what and who God is. "God is invisible and therefore not there." "God is weak because when people call upon Him He rarely answers, so, He must be washed up as God." "Real men and real women don't need anyone to depend upon to control life and its problems." So we quote the soap-opera-special.... "I can take care of myself!" Yeah, right!

Can you stop the sun from coming up in the morning? Can you keep the sun from going down in the evening? Are these really just phenomena of the big bang? Can you change anyone's heart? Oh, maybe you can affect his or her behavior, but can you really change someone's heart? Can you change your own heart? If you are the best one to handle your problems, are you at peace with yourself? Do you struggle at all? You don't? Could that be because you keep pushing out the thoughts of anxiety with denial or compulsive activity?

You wanted to control your own life and destination. God in His grace will let you continue. But He will also increase pressure and pain to get your attention because He never designed you to be able to handle life in your own strength. I have discovered that some people are so fearful and stubborn that they will actually stand in God's face, denounce His power, and proclaim their own ability. Until you come to the point that attempting to exercise your own control is more frightening to you than risking giving up total control to God, you will remain unchanged, or worse. The choice is yours.

So, you wanna be boss? Then continue to trust in yourself who created nothing. Trust in yourself who has a limited view of the future and of the consequences of your actions today. But if you are getting tired of being where the buck stops, consider that there may be more to a relationship with God than you currently understand. If you are more afraid of staying like you are than the unknown of surrendering total control to God, then you are close to experiencing real peace and rest-even if your circumstances get worse!

You think that you are in control but control from your strength is an illusion. The more you try to control, the more you will be controlled by events and people or your own emotions. Continue to attempt to control life in your own strength or surrender control to God. It's your choice.

26

THE PILOT WITHIN

A pilot once told me that today's commercial aircraft are so sophisticated that the pilots don't really fly the plane, they simply monitor it. The pilot locks the plane's computer onto a chosen landing sight and then the plane is drawn to the runway by the computer. The pilot only flies, or controls the plane when it takes off and when it lands. The computer does everything in between, like having a built-in pilot within the plane.

Taking off with an established destination is the pilot's choice. Being in Christ is like riding in a computerized jetliner. Once we chose Christ (something we do as an act of our will), we have an established destination where we will eventually land and that is heaven.

We can get caught up in trying to control or fly our own lives. Even if we could fly a plane accurately, what kind of shape would we be in when we arrived at our destination? I know I would be stressed and exhausted! It makes sense to trust the computer within a plane to get us to our destination. Likewise, it makes sense to trust the pilot within us to get us to our destination. But this asks us to risk trusting Christ to carry us through our lives, through the sunny weather and the storms. He is the plane and the computer.

God doesn't desire us to try and do what He is able and also intends to do. We are too inexperienced to pilot our own lives through the calm or turmoil we face on this earth. To pilot my own life means to me that I am still taking the responsibility of choosing between what I perceive to be good or evil for me; the best path, only accepting obstacles that I feel I can handle. I am trying to guide my own life to the destination I want, using the route I desire, not necessarily what God has filed in His flight plan.

Are you discovering that you are trying to pilot your life? Will you let go of the controls, even if you and God are headed in the same direction? If we made a choice to receive Christ with the resulting destination of actually being in God's presence forever, can't we trust Him to pilot us and land us there safely?

27

IS YOUR FAITH LIVING OR DORMANT?

Most of us do not act on even half of what we know to be true. Often our actions are based on misbeliefs, which are lies and half-truths, or the strong feelings that are attached to our misbeliefs.

Faith without expression is only an intellectual faith. The issue is not whether faith is real but whether or not the faith is living, active, dead, or dormant. The proof of faith shows up in our actions. Our actions betray our beliefs.

How can you be certain of true faith? Examine your heart, your outward expression of life. True faith is confirmed when there is full surrender to God, never thinking of that surrender as a means to manipulate God to give you what you want. This is a give to get mentality.

Actions are the voice of faith. What are your actions saying? Do they say, "I trust you God, no matter how I feel or what my circumstances look like because you are the only one truly trustworthy and faithful?" Or are your actions screaming, "I don't trust You, God, to handle this one?" Or maybe your actions are saying, "I won't risk trusting Christ as my protector. I refuse to relinquish control. I don't believe God has met all my needs in Christ Jesus. God is not enough to satisfy me in this life. I can't trust God with my children. How can I trust when I can't be sure of the outcome? God hates me. God will let me down. God doesn't care. The abundant life is only for those who behave better than me."

What makes you righteous? Does acting on it or simply receiving Christ's righteousness by faith make you righteous? Does acting as if you are righteous make you righteous? No. Receiving makes you righteous. Can I be righteous and not experience it? The answer is, yes. How can I experience more of having been made righteous with His righteousness? By faith, risking that it is true. Step out, make choices, yield yourself to the truth that you are made righteous with His righteousness. Surrender yourself totally to God for Him to break your faith in and reliance on anything other than Him.

28

In Proper Order

Are you putting the cart before the horse? Are you focusing on doing the work of God or are you focusing on having an intimate relationship with Him? Are you trying to drum up passion for the cause but find you can't? It may be because you've not given priority to having an intimate relationship with God.

Until you've given yourself completely to Him, you can't really know His heart and desires for you and His plan for your life. Your first priority should be to give yourself totally to Him. When your passion is God, then it won't matter where He leads you, what He has you doing, or for how long He has you doing it. He'll lead you to His work and sustain it into eternity with an overflow of His life pouring into you and into your work.

Putting the cause of Christ before an intimate relationship with Christ will be empty and unfulfilling in the long run. Let go of anything you are holding on to and take hold of Him. You will find yourself unable to resist where His life leads you to serve in the body of Christ and you will find a passion to serve that comes from a desire to obey the One with whom you are impassioned.

Jesus said to him,
"I am the way, and the truth,
and the life; no one comes to
the Father, but through Me.
If you had known Me, you
would have known My Father
also; from now on you know
Him, and have seen Him."
Philip said to Him, "Lord,
show us the Father, and it
is enough for us." Jesus said
to him, "Have I been so long
with you, and yet you have
not come to know Me, Philip?
He who has seen Me has seen
the Father; how do you say,
show us the Father."

John 14:6-9

29

Don't You Know Me?

How do you get to know someone? How do you come to hear with their ears and see with their eyes and to know how they perceive life around them? You would need to sort of get inside them, wouldn't you? In June 1992 a couple from Germany came to live with us for three months while they attended training classes at the ministry where I worked. When they arrived, several of their expectations were immediately dashed. They loved mornings, cozy breakfasts of certain foods, fresh air and bright sunlight. Linda and I would barely grunt at each other in the morning and didn't eat breakfast. We also had to keep the windows and doors closed with the air conditioning on constantly to shut out the humidity that resulted in mold that could make your walls and clothes fuzzy within three days.

As for the sunlight, we lived in the swag of a neighborhood with trees so thick and tall that you literally had to drive out of our neighborhood to the secondary road to see what kind of day it was. Every day our friends would ask us questions about things we always took for granted, questions that would never have occurred to us to ask because of how ordinary and familiar we are with our country, culture and lifestyle. As a result of their questions, Linda and I began to notice things about our country, our town, our neighborhood, and our church that we had never before noticed. We began to see things through their eyes and hear through their ears. Discount coupons, all-you-can-eat restaurants, mailbox flags, kudzu, muscle cars, tractor-trailers, siren sounds, and Southern cooking were all new or challenging to them, especially the kudzu.

Linda and I learned that without input from another source we would always see things through our own grid of knowledge and understanding. Our grid comes through our experiences. So, what happens if what you think you're seeing isn't true? Would you want to know? Is it wise to make decisions based only on what I see the way I see it? "Have I been so long with you, and yet you have not come to know Me, Philip?"

So, how do you come to know God, I mean really know Him? Well, first you must receive Him to yourself by inviting Him in. Linda and I would not have known our friends unless they had approached us. Is God, through Christ, approaching you, to dwell in you and to take up residence in you? When we first met our German friends it was a risk to invite them into our home. We didn't understand their lifestyle or what they would bring into our lives.

It is a risk to invite God, through Christ, into your life especially if your concept of Him is negative. But is your concept of Him true? Is it built on the expectations and failures of other relationships? If you have expectations of God that weren't fulfilled, the disappointment from this forms your image of Him. To have your concept of God change is not so much a seeking in your own strength but an inviting, a surrendering of our will to His. If your concept is really ugly, this will be a major risk decision.

The first step to know Him is to invite Him into your home; that is your being. The second step is to invite Him into your daily life; that is your waking up in the morning until you go to bed for the night. Take Him with you consciously. He's already there in actuality but we don't experience Him because we aren't looking for Him. We didn't consciously take Him with us to work, to school, to play and, believe it or not, we sometimes won't bring Him to church either. So, how do you come to really know Him? You would need to sort of get inside Him, wouldn't you?

As Jesus is giving the disciples a picture of who God is in John 14, He gives us that same picture in verse 20, *In that day you shall know that I am in My Father, and you in Me, and I in you.* This means that anything that comes into our lives has to first go through the Father and through Jesus before it ever gets to us. Then when it gets to us it finds us full of Jesus. Did you know that you are in God through Christ? Did you know that you are really that secure? Are you experiencing the peace that knowing this brings?

Most people would rather go to a seminar about God than to actually get to know God. Why? Because going to a seminar doesn't require us to change. But if we begin to actually know God on a consistent basis, we risk being changed. Sometimes we fear what changes this would bring. Are you disappointed with what you know about God and the way you perceive Him to deal with and value your issues? What is your perspective of God?

In 1973 I received Christ as my Savior. As time grew I came to know Him as Lord, but I couldn't perform what I saw in the Bible. Eight years later I began to know Christ as Life and my concept of God began to change. That is when I began to have true peace in my life. That is when all I thought I understood God to be as Savior and Lord came into focus. Understanding Christ being my life set me free to see life through His eyes, hear through His ears, and respond with His life flowing through me.

Linda and I were willing to risk inviting our German friends into our home and then into our daily routine and we began to experience life through their eyes and their ears. We risked inviting God into our hearts and then into our daily lives. Having surrendered our wills and our perceived need to control to Him, we began to see with His eyes and hear with His ears. If you haven't received Christ into your heart, I invite you to do so today. If you know Him as Savior only, or maybe you feel you are struggling to serve Him as Lord and you are considering the risks of change that might come from knowing Him as life, I encourage you to take that risk. It's worth it.

30

TO MY DAD
(ONE WITH EACH OTHER)

Though in heaven you may be
I've never felt you closer to me.
I miss the warmth of your loving touch.
Your eyes, your voice, I miss you so much!

But knowing your frame I cannot view,
Caused search for ways to be close to you.
So, from God's Word He made me aware
Of a truth that you and I both share.

We're one with Him. His life we possess.
In this lone truth my soul can rest.
If we're one with Him, we're one with each other.
In Christ we live, right now, together!

One day again we'll be face to face,
When I, too, leave earth having finished my race.
Until then, Dad, keep singing His praises
'Till I'm consciously there in the heavenly places.

*"God is our refuge and strength
a very present help in trouble."*
Psalm 46:1

31

A VERY PRESENT HELP

It started out as a typical Sunday morning at church. I had been teaching the 35-to-40 year-old Sunday school class for a couple of years. That morning, like previous Sunday mornings, the room was filled with people who always seemed to enjoy the class. Each Sunday before I began teaching the lesson I asked the class if they had any prayer requests. Usually, the requests were for a grandma's illness, someone's new job, a couple's new baby or an upcoming mission trip. But this Sunday turned out to be one I would never forget.

I asked if there were any prayer requests and a woman in the back began to speak. "I have a friend whose child has just been diagnosed with spinal meningitis. The child may die and our kids may be in danger too."

Another woman said, "My friend has an adopted child who is 12 years old. He has been fed through a stomach tube since he was two. When this child was living with his birth mother, he was fed Drano and it destroyed his esophagus. He is suddenly having flash-backs of what his mother did to him. He is terrified and my friend, the adopted mom, is asking prayer for him."

A man in the back spoke next. "My son told me that he doesn't want to live with me and his mom any more. He left home this weekend." At that he began to weep.

Then a lady on my left jumped up and ran out of the room. Her husband, holding back tears said, "My son from my first marriage has given my wife grief since he was little because he got it in his mind that I left his mom to marry her. He thought she was to blame for breaking up his home. I didn't even know her then. This has brought much pain and anxiety to her when my son would visit. Well, he is 19 now and realizes more of the truth and has made several attempts to make amends but because she has been so deeply hurt, she can't deal with it emotionally." My wife, Linda, and one of the other women in the class immediately went out to find and comfort the woman.

To my right was a man who had recently started attending the class. Sometimes he brought his pre-teen daughter with him but that day he was by himself looking anxious and disheveled. He said, "I'm supposed to have my little girl with me today but my ex-wife is trying to keep me from her and wouldn't let me have her this week. My ex-wife has a boyfriend and she keeps throwing him in my face." He paused, then said, "And I've got a shotgun and I've got more than one shell."

Okay. If you're the teacher of this class, what do you do? Do you say a short prayer and go on with the lesson as planned somehow pretending that you didn't hear what you just heard? No!

I searched inside where Christ is one with my

spirit, listening for His direction. Unable to move or think, I knew I had to speak. All eyes were fixed on me with that, "What are you going to do?" look.

I glanced down at the floor where I had put my teaching materials, looked back up at the class and said, "Folks, we've got more going on here than a Sunday school lesson is going to fix. We're going to pray. And if it runs over into church time, if anybody needs to leave for choir or anything, you feel free to do so. But we're going to pray."

I got up from my chair, sat down next to the man with the absent pre-teen daughter and put my arms around him. I held him gently, but firmly, as I didn't want him to leave the room in case he was intending to go back to his ex-wife's house.

After an awkward moment of silence, people began to pray. They prayed for the needs that had been brought to our attention as well as others that had not been mentioned. People began to travail in prayer for each other as God moved in their hearts. There were more than 30 people in that room and all but four or five prayed out loud for each other.

After we had prayed well into the morning, spontaneous praise to God for His ability to handle such insurmountable situations rang out in word and song. When all was finished, I didn't know what would happen next. Would people just get up and leave? Would they go straight to the service, hear a sermon, and go home?

Neither of those two scenarios happened. People who had become acquainted with each other primarily through attending the class went up to the people for whom they had prayed. They exchanged phone numbers and invited each other to Sunday dinner so that they could further comfort one another in their pain. There were offers to spend time with each other later in the week and to accompany one another as they sought help for their circumstance. They left the class that day arm in arm and bonded in love.

I thought to myself, "That's what church is about. Children of the Father lifting each other up to Him and ministering to each other's needs."

Listen very carefully to what God said to the Psalmist in Psalm 46:10. *Cease striving and know that I am God; I will be exalted among the nations, I will be exalted in the earth.*

If you are ready to cease striving and bring your matters to the Lord, if your heart is crying out for you to pray for yourself, others, your church or the lost, now is the time to make that prayer known to God.

32

A FINAL ENCOURAGEMENT

Easter will always remind me of childhood egg hunts at my Pawpaw's house. I remember folks all dressed up at church, visits from family who lived out of state, eight millimeter cameras humming, having to stay dressed up Sunday longer than a boy thought was normal, big dinners and long naps. Easter was always quite a day, but my memories of Easter are much different than that of say, Peter, James, and John of the Bible.

Only days before, all hopes were dashed. Terror and uncertainty replaced the confidence that once reigned. Then came Mary to where they had all gathered in the Upper Room. Mary exclaimed, "He isn't there! He has risen! Go see where He once lay!" Could it be? Could Jesus be alive? How? Did someone steal His body? Was it a trick?

Jesus has been crucified, buried, and raised to never die again, Jesus defeated sin and death on our behalf. He died for me to pay the penalty of my sins. I died with Him so that sin's control and power over me is broken and so that I too may walk in newness of life. Yes, I have been raised up with Him and am seated with Him in the heavenly places. It is a done deal. That inheritance happens once we receive Jesus Christ as our Lord and Savior, it is ours by placing the faith He gave us back onto Him. We receive a gift that is unequaled.

Yes, I'll cherish my childhood memories of Easter but I cherish other memories more; the day I said "yes" to Jesus, the day I understood Him living in and through me, the day I understood what it means to be in Him, and the day He called me to tell others. I was encouraged lately by a friend who told me what it meant to him for me to have spent some of my life with him in times gone by. His memory of those times was a great encouragement to me. Let me encourage you to encourage others by sharing what they've meant to you in your spiritual journey. They may not know.

From Linda:

Though others saw it, Ray may not have known how much he meant to everyone that his life touched and what an influence he was in their lives. But there is no doubt that he is fully aware of that now. He has seen his life totally through the eyes of the Father and has heard Him say, "Well done, good and faithful servant."

He has left quite a legacy. I pray that the words in this book have encouraged you in your walk with God. As you experience life in Christ, seeing the truth of who He is and what He desires to do in and through you, that you too, will carry on this legacy, influencing the lives of those around you.

A Final Encouragement

If having a personal relationship with God is a mystery to you, if you have never given your life to Christ and received the new life He has for you, I pray that you will read on. The final words in this book are from Ray, inviting you to experience this life that is offered to you through the gift of Jesus Christ.

Faith means to risk believing something you can't prove. Faith is to risk believing that God's judgment and wrath on sin is real, that Jesus' death, burial, and bodily resurrection is real and that God's love for you is real. If you receive Jesus by faith, He has promised to save you and live inside you forever. God through Jesus Christ, through the Holy Spirit of Him who died and rose again, will make Himself one with your spirit and you will never be the same. He makes our spirit brand new and gives us His life in our spirit from which to face this world with all its joys and trials. This life, when embraced, is free from being controlled by the world's circumstances no matter what comes at us during our time on this planet.

Does that interest you? Or is your current life so good that you think it can meet all your needs forever? Man has fooled himself into thinking that if he does enough good things or at least one really good thing that he will be with God in the end. That isn't the way it works. Salvation and heaven can't be earned, they are free gifts so you can't bargain with God for them. Doing good is great but it doesn't produce or give us God's life, which is what saves us. Salvation isn't about whether you are good enough, it's about whether or not you have His life in you.

The account of creation in Genesis chapter two mentions two trees in the Garden of Eden. The names of these trees are critical to understand salvation is a gift gotten by faith (risking with God). One tree is named "the tree of the knowledge of good and evil." The other tree is named "the tree of Life." Notice that the full name of the first tree is both good and evil. Good and evil were on the same tree. The failure to understand this fact has deceived a lot of people into thinking they are spiritually okay when they really aren't. Here's the deal.

If you are doing the very best you can every day and you are even sorry for the times when you hurt others, this won't give you life. But good and life are not on the same tree. This Life is a gift. You must give up doing good for the purpose of trying to make yourself acceptable to God. This is performance based acceptance and the Kingdom of God doesn't work that way. It was never designed to work that way. True goodness that comes from His Life is found only by believing in Jesus Christ and the payment He paid on the cross; dying, being buried and resurrecting on the third day.

But, hey, you are free to keep on trying. Let me share one tidbit of info that you really need to know. The Bible also says that "the law makes nothing perfect" (Hebrews 7: 19). What does that mean? It means that you can do all the right things the right way at the right time even for the right reasons, but it won't make you perfect enough to miss hell and get into heaven. It won't make you perfect enough to get His life. You can't earn it. You can keep every law of God, every law of man, every tradition of your family and culture and every law of your particular religion (yes, even your religion), but this won't give you life. The Bible says that the person who has the Son has the life and the person who does not have the Son of God does not have the life. It's just that simple.

If you are beginning to understand this, if you really get this, what prevents you from dropping your guard and receiving Christ as your Savior right now? Hey, tomorrow is not promised. Yesterday is gone. All you have is this moment. So, what do you say? It's simple. Tell God that you realize that you are sinful and have sinned and that you need Jesus; that you've been living off the "tree of the knowledge of good and evil" (your way), and want to exchange it for the gift of the "tree of Life" (Jesus).

Tell Him that by faith (faith, because you can't see it, hear it, feel it) you risk believing that Jesus Christ, God's own Son, came to earth and paid for your sins and sinfulness on the cross; that you now understand that Jesus satisfied the debt of your sin. Tell Him that by faith you believe that Jesus Christ died and rose again three days later.

Now. Here's where the rubber meets the road. Tell Him that by a conscious choice of your will, by the faith that He's given you, "I now receive Jesus Christ as my Savior, Lord, and my very Life." The Bible says that if you believe this in your heart you will become right with God and if you confess it out loud, you will know that you are saved.

Congratulations! If you did this from your heart, you are now His spiritual child forever. You have been reborn spiritually into a new family, His family, with new spiritual DNA! God will now start you on a journey from where you are in your current understanding of Him to an intimate relationship experience with this living God who deeply loves and values you. Welcome to the family!

ABOUT
HIGHER IMAGE MINISTRIES

After serving in youth ministry at our hometown church in Gainesville, GA, for nine years and sixteen years doing Christian counseling, teaching, and training with Grace Ministries offices in Marietta, Georgia, Budapest Hungary, and Manassas, Virginia, Ray and I established Higher Image Ministries in 2002. Soon afterward a sudden illness resulted in Ray's graduation from this life to his life in Heaven with God. As I continue the ministry we began together I realize that with Ray's absence some things will be different but I know the message will be the same. I have made myself available to go where God provides opportunities to speak and share the story of our journey and Father's love and faithfulness.

My life's journey has taken me to the mountain tops as well as to some very deep valleys - struggles in marriage, battles with cancer, the loss of my wonderful husband. In one of those valleys in 1981, God revealed a life-changing truth to both my husband and me - the truth of our new identity in Christ. We began to discover the depths of God's grace and His unconditional love and it transformed every area of our lives. Growing deeper in these truths over the years enables me to trust Father as I face all that is in my life each moment. As Father continues to conform me to the image of Christ, I find that His grace really is sufficient, even through the valleys.

If this book encourages you in your journey I would love to hear from you. You can write me at the addresses below.

Higher Image Ministries is a nonprofit, Christian, cross-denominational, teaching, and personal growth ministry helping people find life in Christ. The message of God's grace and who we really are as His children can unwrap the gift of an abundant, victorious life given to us by our Heavenly Father. Sharing that message with others is the heartbeat of Higher Image Ministries.

This ministry exists to assist local churches and groups in encouraging and equipping people to walk in a personal, intimate relationship with God. Linda does this through speaking and music. The schedule can be designed to meet the needs of the host group.

CONTACT

Higher Image Ministries, Inc.
P. O. Box 809
Flowery Branch, GA 30542
Phone/Fax: 770-967-7778
Email: info@higherimage.org
www.higherimage.org

NOTES

Chapter 19

[1] Dunn, Ronald, *Don't Just Stand There, Pray Something*, (Nashville, TN: Thomas Nelson Inc.), 1992, p. 144.

Chapter 23

[1] Holley, Al, *Nearer To Me*, (Douglasville, GA: written and recorded by Al Holley on the album *We Won't Be Here Long*), 1982.